The Tennis Psychologist

Psychology for Club Players and Captains

ADRIAN LOBLEY

ISBN: 1482383284
ISBN-13: 978-1482383287

Cover design by Jasmin

This book is dedicated to my family and friends and all the tennis players I have enjoyed playing with over the years. Thank you all for such great times. Special thanks to mum for your assistance on the book

TABLE OF CONTENTS

1 INTRODUCTION

WHAT THIS BOOK IS ABOUT

Tennis matches can often be decided by a player who has a particular strength which gives him an advantage over his opponent. Typical examples include having a strong serve, being fast or having great stamina. Are you a player who doesn't feel you have a particular strength, would love to have one but doesn't know how to go about getting one? Or are you someone who has a number of attributes that give you an advantage but would like more for example? Then this book is for you. There is an extra dimension that I can provide you with. That extra dimension is to utilise your mind to its maximum.

This book teaches you how to out think your opponent, how to put doubt in his head and make him question his own game. It works towards mentally strengthening your own mind and improving your match play. It is not concerned with coaching or teaching you how to play tennis shots, the only reference to playing shots relates to the way you construct a point by thinking about your shots, i.e. the mental side.

Most tennis books concentrate on how to play tennis explaining stroke play and positioning and these books often include perhaps only one chapter dealing with the mental side of tennis. As these books are aimed at providing an all-round summary of the game they do not delve at all deeply into the enormous topic of tennis psychology which is the subject examined here.

This book is essentially targeted at players who play club tennis and who play in teams although will be of interest to beginners and professionals alike. As a large amount of club play is centred around playing doubles then this book is written with doubles play in mind and also team match play however many of the principles can be used for singles as well.

There are a great many books on the market that deal with sports psychology and a small number that specialise in tennis psychology. Most of these books cover every mental weakness that can be thought of and show how to overcome them. The drawback with teaching in this way is that you are putting new ideas of possible weaknesses and worries into your reader's head which he may previously not have thought of. This book tries to minimise thoughts of negativity and concentrate on positive aspects.

Most books touching on the subject of tennis psychology are written by professional tennis players who have been at the top of the game. However it is likely that you are similar to me in that you have not played at that level and in fact play in a different world to this at your local club. What you need to know is not necessarily what works at a professional level but what works at a local level. The concerns and neuroses of the local tennis player are not always the same as the tennis professional. I have studied the local club and team player for over twenty five years and therefore have a lot of useful information to impart to you.

WHY THE MENTAL SIDE OF TENNIS IS SO IMPORTANT

Tennis is one of the most mentally challenging sports there is. In team games such as football, rugby and hockey there are many more players to share the mental burden. In other individual games such as snooker and squash players have not got the elements such as sun, wind and rain to contend with and other sports such as darts and badminton, the tricky aspect of topspin, backspin or sidespin does not exist. For these reasons tennis is a wonderful challenge and you will need every positive, logical and sensible idea you can lay your hands on. These can all be found here.

RUNNING A TEAM

There are two chapters in this book on running teams. At some point in your tennis 'career' it is highly likely that you will either volunteer or be volunteered to run a team. There is a fair amount of work involved and your phone bill will probably increase but there are also definite bonuses namely that you get to play as often as you want and with who you want and there can also be a great feeling of achievement in winning silverware or finishing higher than anyone thought you could.

There are a huge number of psychological mind games that you can employ as a captain of a team and many tricks of the trade. This is the first book to dedicate time to the subject of the psychology of tennis captaincy and if nothing else it will amuse you to see the different kinds of tricks you can employ.

BACKGROUND OF WHERE THE CONTENT CAME FROM

This book has been a culmination of twenty five years tennis playing experience, of playing at many clubs with and against a huge variety of players: good, bad, old, young, talented, wily, angry, calm, winners, losers, good looking and not so good looking. The content of this book comes from studying them, watching what they do and listening to what they say.

I wrote the vast majority of this book from just tapping into the information stored in my head as I was keen to make my conclusions from experiences that I knew to be true. In other words I was keen for the foundation of the book to be based on real life. Once I had laid the foundation, I then researched the thinking and findings of established professionals with regard firstly to general psychology and then secondly to tennis psychology. Having researched general psychology it was interesting to take the scenarios which were given and apply those to the tennis player. Typical general areas included dealing with anger and increasing positive thinking.

Having carried out a great deal of research I found that writings on tennis psychology were often explained at a theoretical level, which of course is key, however the reader was expected to translate that theory to the court without being shown examples of what should be done. In this book we look at both the theoretical side but also the practical side, i.e. what to do to get that psychological advantage on court.

As this book was written over a fair period of time, I had the opportunity to retest over and again the theories and practices that I had written about, by taking the piece of advice onto the court to check it worked. If it didn't then it didn't make it into the book. As it is often difficult to remember all the points that are explained as you go through the book, it helps to be able to focus on and remember the key points, so these have been highlighted at the end of each chapter. This should improve the chance of them appearing in your head on court once you have read the book. I would still recommend though that you read each chapter rather than just skipping to the summary. The summaries can then be reviewed just before you go on court.

Throughout this book I have abbreviated 'he/she' to 'he'.

THE AIM OF THE BOOK

The aim of this book is to give you that 10% on the court that you wouldn't have had before reading this book and give you a weapon that your opponent does not have. This means that it will be easier to beat players who are the same standard as you and make it possible to beat those who you have always considered to be a little better than you.

What this book will also teach you though is that there is a lot more to tennis psychology than you had probably realised and that is why it is such a fascinating topic. By the end of the book I hope you will find the excitement of the tennis mind games just as much fun as the game itself.

2 KEEPING QUIET AND LISTENING TO THE OPPOSITION

LISTENING TO THE OPPOSITION

How different would it be if you could actually read your opponent's mind on court? Imagine a tennis match where you know all your opponent's fears and concerns, you know whether he believes he can beat you and what his weaknesses are and even where he is going to place his next shot. This utopian ideal might not be fully achievable but as you read on you will be surprised at how far down the road you can actually go to knowing another person's mind on court.

So how do we go about finding out this information? We have to look at how else (other than actual mind reading) we are going to gather this information and also maximise the amount we can gather. There are two ways to do this:

- Your opponent tells you his weaknesses
- Your opponent's team-mates tell you about

your opponent's weaknesses

Let's look at both of these in turn.

YOUR OPPONENT TELLS YOU HIS WEAKNESSES

You may ask how you are going to get an opponent to tell you his weaknesses but it is surprising what he does actually tell you. You just need to listen. You also need to train your team-mates to listen and communicate any useful information. The most common way of course is during the match he will often make exclamations criticising his weakest shot such as 'my backhand is useless'. Fairly obvious from comments like this, where you need to aim on crunch points.

In the past after a match I once had an opponent say to me how she struggled when I hit a high kicking shot to her backhand. She presumably believed that as the match had finished, it wouldn't alter the result. This was true but what she didn't consider was that I would be playing against her for many years to come, twice a year. I have to admit remembering it so well because it was such a good example of what not to say. It actually made me even more eager to play against her as I wanted to test out the new information.

Another example was playing a set against a friend and being 5-2 down. I was working on a particular shot at the time and my goal was more to improve this rather than win the match. For this reason I didn't alter my game at all but surprisingly ended up winning 7-5. My opponent said to me afterwards "I've never beaten you and I don't have the belief that I can". This is an example of how psychological a game of tennis can be and that it wasn't totally obvious to me when playing him that his mind was in this state but I would know for future.

YOUR OPPONENT'S TEAM-MATES TELL YOU ABOUT YOUR OPPONENT'S WEAKNESSES

In some matches not all the players on the two teams will be playing all the time, there may be periods where players are sitting off, for example if one court finishes earlier than the other or if it is a three couple match but there are only two courts. Whilst sitting off court your opponents will chat to their team-mates and will discuss their own shots, their own injuries and their team-mates' weaknesses as they watch them play. Just make sure you sit close enough to hear. Opposition spectators can be particularly garrulous and can also be subtly tapped for information and it is amazing how much they will reveal.

If you are captain you need to instruct your team to listen out as you will not always be off court yourself.

In the same way you and your team-mates must make sure none of these things are done by yourselves or your spectators.

The most information that is provided by the opposition is usually to your team's best player as human nature with a lot of people is to try and befriend the best player or at least engage him in conversation. The more a person talks, the more he reveals.

I recently entered a mixed doubles tournament that was for pairs from around the region who were entering on behalf of their club. As none of our club's ladies were available that day I entered with a strong girl from a rival club. As it happened we were due to play her team a couple of weeks later in the cup final and so she asked me who was going to be playing for my team in the final. All the time in the conversation I was having with her I was at maximum concentration to ensure I gave away no vital information but wanted also to be able to pick up on any she might let slip. I answered her question by saying "the usual gang" so I didn't give away too much information but also answered the question – after all she was partnering me in the tournament as a favour so I certainly didn't want to be rude. I asked her then who would be playing for her team and she named all six players. The next ploy I used was to express surprise about two of the three men that were playing. In actual fact all three men she had picked were undoubtedly their best three men so it was a good choice on her part. However she was aware of their weaknesses better than I was as she played with them regularly. When I expressed surprise her natural human reaction was the same as anyones, a bit of a resigned sigh and then an explanation of their weaknesses, "yes it depends which Dave and John turn up on the day and whether they start arguing". Mental note to not let these guys get a good start in the cup final a few weeks later and to put them against our strongest players first in order to get them off to a bad start.

READING BETWEEN THE LINES

You also need to be able to read between the lines. I have an extremely good mixed doubles partner and when arriving first at the opposition ground I was asked by the opposition captain, with a resigned sigh, "is your girl playing tonight?". This was music to my ears. The opposition captain clearly feared my tennis partner. When she arrived, the first thing I said to her was "they fear you, the opposition captain is worried about playing you, he's just told me". Everyone likes to know opponents are scared of playing them, it gives them a boost.

Even an insult can be a compliment. I was surprised to see a county standard men's doubles player playing in a match in our mixed league. We had had a particularly long rally, the result of which I can't remember – it could have gone either way, but he just grumbled under his breath "…..hackers" referring to me just rallying endlessly. This was good to hear as I made sure I kept the rallies going as long as I could, doing everything I could to keep the ball in, just to wind him up more and more.

Whilst playing in a different match an opponent said "You always make me run – I'm knackered after playing you". This immediately stamped a permanent goal in my head for the future that meant every time I played him again I wanted to make him run as much as possible to try and get him to say those words again to me.

THE NERVOUS BEGINNER

When a player plays his first match he is usually nervous and often talks non-stop about how nervous he is and how poor he thinks he is. If you are partnering such a player then as his partner it is up to you to tell him to say nothing negative and instruct him that when he is on court he must do everything he can to portray the illusion that not only is he not nervous but that he is a confident player. When he is due to stand at the net, despite perhaps being wary about being positioned there, he needs to punch the volleys with confidence and attack the ball. All he needs to do is make one good strong volley early on and the opposition will more often than not keep the ball away from him at the net. Display weakness however and the opposition will seize on it. If your partner does miss the first shot then a made up exclamation from him of, "I never miss those", is worth a try. If you are the more experienced player then make these suggestions to your partner.

EXCUSES

Another part of keeping quiet is with regard to excuses. Most circumstances are the same for your opponents as well as yourself, e.g. sun in eyes, wind, slippery courts. A method worth trying if you are team captain is to ban your team from making any negative comments because once the negative comments start they tend to multiply.

If you are aware of an opponent's injuries (whether someone has told you or you recall it happening) then a slightly devious technique is to ask your opponent how his injury is before you play him. Doing this brings the injury to the forefront of your opponent's mind just before the start of the match. Most people like to play to the audience and so if a player starts losing, an injury is an excellent excuse for him, so he begins to exaggerate the injury and will then rarely do well as his focus is not on the next point but on his performance in front of the gallery. The gallery of course may just be his partner and the opposition. Although a rather sly idea, you are not causing any injury, purely helping yourself to an advantage over your opponent who will be none the wiser.

On the flip side if you are to get an injury then you should try to disguise this fact and if anyone mentions it try not to even acknowledge it, just change the subject immediately to a subject other than injuries.

One idea I tried in a tournament was to try to plant 'a seed of an excuse' into an opponent's head. The tournament was divided into two groups with the winner of each group playing off in a one set final. It was noticeable that my partner and I had been drawn in the easier of the two groups and therefore managed to qualify for the final without expending too much energy on what was a hot day. In the other group however the eventual winners had much longer, tougher matches and ended up playing more games.

As we exchanged pleasantries with our opponents prior to the final starting I commented to the lady opponent that I felt they had a much harder group and must be exhausted and that it didn't seem that fair as they had had to play more games than us. She immediately responded, as you would expect, saying that it wasn't a problem as she was feeling quite fresh.

Our opponents started off very well leading 4-1 and 40-0 in the one-set final. We then managed to lift our game and our opponents' fire started to lessen. We managed to come back to win 6-4.

The change I believe was due to two factors, we found a slight weakness in the man's game and played on that and secondly the lady seemed to tire.

Now without actually asking the opposition lady why her game went off we have no idea of the actual reason. It might be that she was genuinely tired or that pressure affected her. However I do wonder whether by planting the seed in her head, i.e. that she had an excuse to lose the match as they had played more games and tougher matches than us, this had affected her in some way. The fact that she felt I was trying to get a psychological advantage may also have added to it.

THE RE-ARRANGED MATCH

A few years ago our team had a title clash against the strongest team in the league. It was a re-arranged match and I was discussing with the opposition captain when she arrived what hard work it was to re-arrange matches. She commented in passing that she hoped the match didn't get rained off again as most of their team were away over the next three weeks. Without her realising it this was a useful piece of information she had given me. The match got under way but before long the rain came down and soon got heavier and heavier until the point when the match had to be abandoned.

As home captain, it was my job to come back to the opposition with three dates when we could play the re-arranged match. As the opposition captain had told me most of her team were away over the next three weeks naturally I did my utmost to come up with three dates that fell during this period, which I managed to do. As it happened in this instance one of the dates suited their players and they got a good team out, however, it is an example that shows how a small amount of information could be quite valuable. It is just about listening to what the opposition tell you.

SUMMARY

It can be seen that the words that you, your teammates, the opposition or either sets of spectators say can have a massive influence on the result of a match. So make sure you and your team listen to what they say and use it to your advantage, and ensure that your team keep their counsel.

3 DEALING WITH AND TAKING ADVANTAGE OF RAGE

Being captain occasionally means you have to deal with players who can cause difficulties. In some cases players' anger levels can be the issue. In this chapter we look at ways of managing their anger and improving the situation.

CONTAINING THE RAGE

There are some players who can't contain their anger and the angrier they get the more points they throw away. This is often the case with juniors and the player who can't contain his rage. I have also seen it happen where an opposition player with a huge ego who has just lost his first set, which he believed he had a right to win, then threw all his remaining sets because of this, causing his team to lose the match.

As a player we want to know how we can use our opponent's anger to our advantage. To get your opponent to throw a match by getting angry, you need to seize your chance as soon as you see him losing control for the first time. The first point following a tantrum is very important. In doubles play, anger in one person can have hidden effects too. Bear in mind, no one who plays doubles enjoys playing with someone who is swearing and throwing his racket. It can put you off and put pressure on your own shots as you think your partner is having a go at you. There are a number of negative things going on at the same time.

The person who gets angry is often the one who has a lot of gremlins in his head. In a match at Wimbledon in 1981 against Tom Gullikson, John McEnroe recalled, "The devils were crawling all over my brain".

The enraged player can have many different thoughts, I have heard one say that when the red mist descends he starts believing that as he has lost the last shot it is likely he will lose the next one. In his head he can have a chain of negative thoughts, not about the past but about the future that, of course, hasn't occurred yet. Tomaz Mencinger comments on his Tennis Mind Game website, "The mind tends to predict".

The great thing about tennis is that if you have just lost a point, regardless of whether it was a bad shot choice or an easy smash missed, if you win the next point then it wipes the bad shot from history (unless it was game point of course).

The players who have bad tempers can often be the stronger tennis players who you would like to have in your team for every match. The difficulty might be though the amount of upset they can cause. The best way round this therefore is to see if there is a way of taming the beast. Possible ways of dealing with people who can't control their temper are as follows:

- If you are the captain then try pairing the player with someone who he has respect for, as he is more likely to control his behaviour as he doesn't want to look foolish in the eyes of someone he looks up to.
- As captain, talk to him about his temper. Discuss ways as to how it can be controlled. The player who loses his temper easily may be trying his hardest not to get angry but it may be part of his nature and discussing it with him might help. Everyone is different and the only way to solve any potential issues is if you are aware of all the facts and can discuss ways of reducing the likelihood of the rage returning.
- In a non-match situation it is a good opportunity to put an angry person with an even angrier person. It may turn bad but ask each player how he felt when his partner got angry. If he said that he didn't enjoy it, then with great tact, explain to him, that is how people feel when they partner him when he is angry.
- As his partner, make a 'guilt-point'. This is just a quick sentence which has an impact on the person receiving the comment. Say to your partner that when he gets angry it upsets you and makes your game deteriorate. Even something as simple as this can have the desired effect.
- The partner of an irate player has a vital role; he is the one who needs to talk to the player during the match to keep him calm. This can often help the player. It does depend on each player

though, hence the need for discussion. If you are the calmer of the two, it is undoubtedly in your interest not to have your partner getting irate.

- So many tennis matches are won by the slightest margin or the slightest event. In professional tournaments we often see the difference a rain delay or even an injury timeout makes. If you feel you are losing control of your temper then why not change something. Pretend you need something from the clubhouse. The fact you are walking, moving to a different place, going from a light place to a dark place perhaps and are cooling down slightly can all have a part to play in calming you down. It's really not sporting doing this more than once or twice in a match but if done at a time when you feel you might be about to explode then saying you have lost your vibration damper and nipping to your car to see if you have a spare one may help you to get back on course.
- When a player is about to explode on court then he needs to find an alternative release. One way is for the player to tap his partner's hand (as you will see the professionals do). In life, in general, the human touch is one of the best ways of relieving stress, such as a handshake. Although handshakes on court are not done mid-match the same principal can be adopted by a quick hand tap which triggers an anger-release. A hand-tap also has other subliminal messages. It increases the bond between the players and puts the thought in the opponent's head that the hand-tapping pair are very much a partnership

and that when one player misses a shot it doesn't upset the other.

- Another useful method of anger release is for the player, who often loses his temper, to put a rubber band on his wrist before the match and ping it when he feels angry. He must train himself to think that whenever either the hand tap or the rubber band actions are taken, all the anger is released and it snaps his concentration back to the game.
- A bad tempered player might keep a damp face cloth in a bag on court and when he is getting hot and bothered wipe his face with the cloth.
- Another technique to induce calm is to use the visual aid of a tennis professional who the player has seen many times on TV and respects. In times of rage he might try to visualise Pete Sampras playing and how calm he was on court. He must let that feeling of calm float into his body.

In an interview on the 'British Tennis Coaches Association' website, Dave Sammell, who is the head coach at the Monte Carlo Tennis Academy, speaks about dealing with juniors, advising, "We have a 'No Moods Allowed' rule which helps them nurture the right attitude in the academy".

If a person does have a problem containing his rage then it can often spiral out of control. The key is to nip it in the bud and ensure that he doesn't even get onto the first rung of the 'angry ladder'.

Sometimes no matter how calm you are as a person you swear before you know it. When you hear your opponent swearing, it is a good feeling as it shows that he is not as assured as he might be appearing. If you must curse therefore it is best to turn your back to the opposition, put your head down and swear without volume.

If Mencinger's following comments are true then his words should give those of you who get angry a great reason for not showing it, "Many get angry but if you listen and observe really carefully you will hear fear underneath. Anger is just the mask. Fear is the original emotion. Fear of losing, fear of being criticised again, fear of loss and so on".

AVOIDING RAGE BY FOCUS

The focus of a player's attention is key in tennis. Between points focus must always be on the next shot you will be playing. If a player's focus is elsewhere, e.g. on the people watching, on the previous point he lost or won, or in the middle of a self-generated rage, then he is seriously hindering his chance of winning the next point.

It is important that your concentration is not on too many things otherwise you will end up not doing the basics. The following questions are the only ones that you should concentrate on. They are few enough that you can remember them but enough so that your focus is brought back to the court and back to the next point.

If you are serving:

- Which spot on the court are you aiming to hit the ball to?
- How hard do you intend to hit the ball?

If you are receiving your next shot:

- Where are the likely places it will be placed?
- Are you stood in the position that will maximise your chance of returning it successfully?

AVOIDING RAGE BY RESPECT

Sometime ago I played a match with a novice. She was in her mid-twenties and had picked up a racket just the year before for the first time and had been having coaching for a year. She agreed to help us out in a match which unfortunately was against the top team in the region. This was always going to be a tough task for us. It was a case of damage limitation particularly against the opposition's top pair and then a case of getting more games on the board against the remaining two pairs. Midway through the match I missed an easy shot which would normally have led to me letting out an exclamation of despair. However, due to this being my partner's first match I managed to suppress the exclamation because I couldn't risk upsetting her as she may have assumed I was blaming her. In the same situation with a different partner I would undoubtedly have shouted something. This means therefore that I am able to control what I shout. As we have established already if I show anger it provides encouragement to my opponents and works to my detriment. However if I can employ the self-control technique I have just learnt, then logic says I can avoid shouting ever again.

The self-control technique we have just learnt is actually to imagine you are playing with the player who you would not want to upset. In some cases this might be a beginner, for some players it might be the best player at the club for whom you have tremendous respect or it might even be someone you are attracted to that you don't want to look like a fool in front of.

A good example of self-control was shown by John McEnroe in his playing days. There was only one opponent against who he never let his rage show, Bjorn Borg. There were two reasons for this, firstly that he knew he was going to need every last bit of energy to beat Borg so he didn't want to use any up getting angry but also because of the amount of respect he had for Borg. This was partly down to the manner in which Borg handled himself around the court – that of a gentleman.

In Malcolm Folley's book 'Borg Versus McEnroe' he quotes Jimmy Connors, "Anything you did on court with Bjorn made you look worse, I always tempered my craziness when I played him. There was no chance of getting inside Bjorn's head".

This is the place where you need to be. It might not be possible to play as well as a professional but you can certainly act and behave as the professionals like Borg do. How good a compliment would it be to hear your opponent say that it is impossible to ruffle your feathers?

AVOIDING ANGER BY NOT LOOKING LIKE A FOOL

Human beings usually enjoy receiving compliments and as a child playing tennis I was no different. On one occasion I lost a match but didn't get angry and was complimented for taking defeat well. This helped in containing my anger for future matches as I enjoyed the compliment. As you get older of course into your late teens, then losing gracefully is expected. If you are close to someone this age who is acting up, and he respects your judgement, then have a word with him as he may not realise he is doing anything wrong and so just needs telling.

If you get into your twenties and are still throwing your racket or getting in a strop then I have news for you – you look like a fool!

HOW TO PREVENT AN OUTBURST

In William Davies' book 'Overcoming Anger and Irritability' he explains that the key areas are: (a) what triggers a person's anger, (b) the anger itself (which can gradually build up, like increasing amounts of water being poured into a bucket), (c) inhibitions (which stop us constantly giving vent to our anger) and (d) the response. He emphasizes that there is no need to 'let our anger out' as this often makes things worse. Better to let it slowly seep away, like water running out of a leaky bucket.

Davies goes onto explain that time length is key to this also. Relating this to tennis, if a player misses three easy shots in a row then the anger builds quickly so the bucket will overflow and an outburst can occur. If however the player misses these three straight forward shots over the course of the set then it is unlikely that the player would have an outburst as his anger would have been given the chance to just seep away on each occasion before the next top up. Often anger can take a player's mind off the next point and can cause more and more easy misses. So if a player can keep his anger in check and concentration high this will hopefully space out the missing of the simple shots and therefore prevent the outburst from occurring.

Davies explains the traffic light principle, "All we have to do is learn to spot a red light! And that's easy. Any amount of irritation or anger we feel is effectively a red light. So we don't just barge across it; that way lies disaster. When confronted by a red light, we stop. Some say 'Count to ten' although you can say anything under your breath or in your mind until the anger has subsided to a tiny amount (the lights change) and you get ready to move on to your next point."

Become razor sharp at recognizing impending irritability and anger and put yourself on red straight away. Think of a person you have set as an example to model yourself and what he would do in this situation. That puts you onto amber and then move onto the next point, i.e. green.

Davies goes onto comment that often anger can come from just being in a bad mood and this can be caused by any number of factors such as poor nutrition, drugs, lack of sleep, illness, lack of routine, stress and social factors. If it's possible to get these factors right then you are much less likely to find yourself in a bad mood. One thing to remember is that if you are feeling irritable because you are stressed out make sure you put the blame fairly and squarely where it belongs, so if it is someone at work who is winding you up, don't displace it onto whoever happens to be closest at hand, i.e. your tennis partner. If you can, then reduce the stresses, learn to cope with them better or view the stresses in a different light. It should also be noted that inhibitions can be developed and worked upon too to reduce the number of times a player will have an outburst.

CHANNELLING YOUR ANGER IN A POSITIVE WAY

There is however an alternative to letting your anger leak away because as we all know that's not always easy to do. It is to channel the anger so it works in your favour.

If someone was to graphically illustrate your level of anger during a match then more often than not it would be largely uniform. The line would generally be straight albeit a gradual upward slant if you are losing or downward if you are winning. Every now and then there would be a spike in the graph when your anger levels would shoot up for example if you feel you have been cheated.

Below we have an example where the player who is losing has had a couple of bad calls go against him in a very short period of time. These are represented by the two spikes. The anger level of the player who made the bad calls, who happens to be winning in this instance, is also shown.

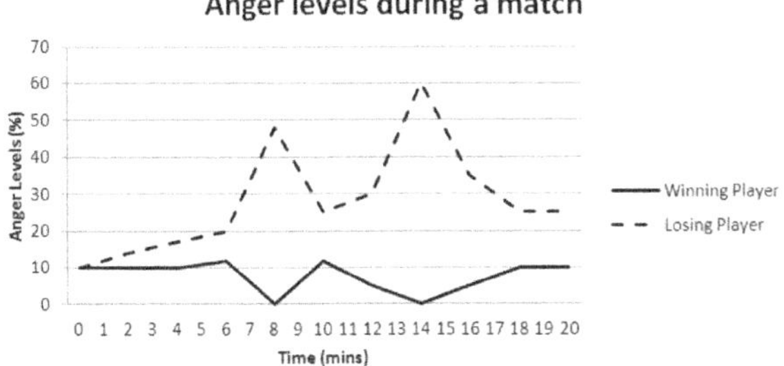

These spikes can be critical. Some players lose the plot totally when they have a bad call against them and will blaze the next few shots out of the back of the court just to make a statement. We hear of people talking about being in the zone when hitting endless winners in a short space of time however what we have here is, the 'anger-zone'.

When in the anger-zone however there is the opportunity to use the adrenalin rush and anger to your own advantage by channelling it. A lot of players are able to use this anger to their advantage, which means if others can, then you can. The anger can drive you into using more power but as long as you can control your strokes in the same way that you would normally you can use your intense feeling to re-ignite your passion for the particular game you are in.

The anger-zone does not last long for most of us because the mind gradually forgets, the anger seeps away with time and also you are likely to win a point before long and start feeling a bit better about yourself. It is often difficult to keep this level of adrenalin and intensity up for a long time but it can win you a lot of points in a short space of time providing the part of your mind which controls the shots is given a say at the time of the adrenalin-rush. If you enter the anger-zone then your mind is effectively consumed with 100% anger. The key is to force some other thought into your mind. One possible way is to adopt a process to reduce the anger.

The process or solution to adopt here is to 'squeeze' the 100% anger you have, reduce it to 90% of the mind's thoughts and force the other 10% to be occupied by 'control'. In doing this your natural instinct is still of overriding anger and you can still take your aggression out on the ball but instead of blazing the ball into the opponent's back netting, you are going to get the ball in court. In this case the way to prevent the ball flying into the opponent's back netting when venting your fury is to apply topspin and so by doing this you have got out your aggression but also given yourself a chance of winning the point. The millisecond between the anger being dissipated by hitting the ball and the point where the topspin is applied the rage is released. If successful it may even prompt you to realise that you can hit the ball harder than you do normally and give you more winning shots in your normal game. The diagram below isn't so much to show the theory but rather to use as a visual aid. Take a mental photograph of it. This will assist in making the idea stick in your mind.

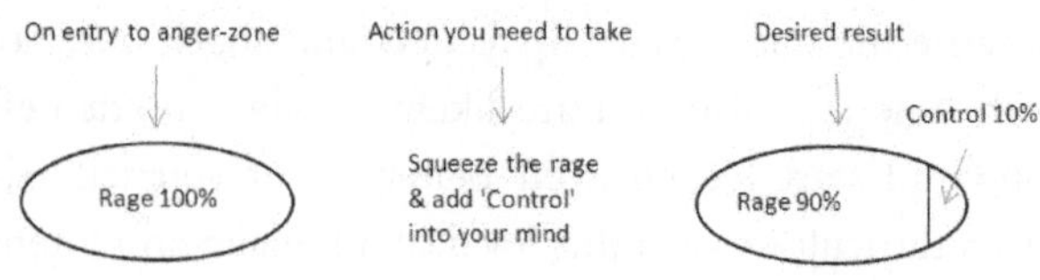

As the anger levels are so high in the first couple of

points after an incident the mind immediately starts monitoring the success rate of your shots from this point and heightens the awareness of whether hitting your shots with anger is reaping better results or not. If however you feel you are unable to apply the control at the end of the shots then the only option is the difficult one, namely to chill as quickly as possible.

To summarise, we are looking here at how we have been able to win points we might normally have lost by using the sudden anger we have, so we are turning the normal result on its head.

BLANKING YOUR MIND

W.Timothy Gallwey in his book 'The Inner Game of Tennis' proposed that when you go on court you are in fact two people namely that you consist of an inner and an outer self. He explains that the inner self is the one who plays the shots and knows perfectly well how to play the shots and if left alone would be able to play them correctly. He adds that there is also an outer self though which is the one who sets the expectations and scolds the inner self if the inner self, who controls the shots, doesn't play them as required. How often do we hear people telling themselves off, this is the outer self having a go at the inner self. Gallwey explains that the best way to success is to work at removing the outer self from the equation altogether. To do this the player needs to blank his mind and trust in his inner self, i.e. play the shot as though on autopilot – after all the inner self knows how to play.

This indeed is a lesson taught by sports psychologists and players can train themselves mentally to achieve the blank mind. Malcolm Folley writes that 'When Bjorn Borg knocked up he made his mind blank and just did drills'.

SUMMARY

- If you are a player that suffers from rage on court then we have covered a number of physical (e.g. hand tap, rubber band, damp face cloth) and psychological ways (e.g. visual imagery of a professional player, moving your focus to where you are going to hit the ball on the next point etc.) to help you control your anger.
- Think about which method works best for you so either slowing things down and letting the anger seep away or alternatively harnessing the anger you have inside you to go all out on the upcoming points in a controlled manner.
- If you are captain of a team which has a player in it who struggles with his temper then try playing him with someone he respects. Also talk to him about the best way he can control his anger.

If you are the partner of a player who can't control his rage then you have a responsibility to do something – don't just stand back and pretend that your partner isn't throwing his racket across the court when he is. Keep talking to him, don't let him play the next point until he has calmed down, i.e. slow things down. Don't let your partner get on the first rung of the 'angry ladder'.

4 THE PSYCHOLOGY OF THAT EXTRA POINT

SECTION 1 - BUILDING THE PSYCHOLOGICAL FOUNDATION

Before we look at the ways of squeezing as many points out of a game as possible it is necessary to get the basics right first. For this we introduce the Psychological Foundation. The Psychological Foundation is made up of three stages. One of these is mental preparation - improving your confidence going into a match. Then the remaining two stages are concerned with what to do during the match. They are fairly obvious areas, however it is amazing how many players do not consider areas such as their opponents' weaknesses, because they are so caught up in their own weaknesses, and also that they do not give themselves the opportunity to play to their own strengths.

STAGE 1 - CREATION OF A CONFIDENCE PLATFORM

When I was younger I played badminton against the number one player in the county on two occasions. I lost the first match 15-3. He was a lot better than me and 15-3 reflected the difference between us accurately. The second time I played him it was heading towards a similar score line as he lead 14-3. I managed to then win the next eight points to pull it back to 14-11 before eventually succumbing, 15-11. I have no doubt that my opponent will have taken his foot off the gas a little as he knew he was home and dry in this second match whereas I was fighting for everything I could get. I can't recall the reason I was trying so hard, it may have been to save face, or to try to win or to show my opponent and my team-mates that I deserved to be on court with the guy or perhaps all of these reasons.

Stepping back from the match itself and analysing just the scores, this example shows the difference in appearance the extra points (or games in tennis) can make when you look back on a result. You often resort to thinking back to how you have done and statistics can mask the facts. What this score line did do was give me a confidence platform for future matches. In my mind I could now adopt the positive mental attitude of, "if I can take eleven points from the best in the county surely I can now beat players who are currently ranked above me but aren't as good as this guy". Effectively I was hiding the fact that the real score line of the second match should perhaps have been 15-3 but by doing this it was a way of boosting my own confidence and as we know in sport (and particularly tennis) confidence is all important.

So the building of a platform is essential. Once you staple certain scores or results into your memory these can create a positive basis when you are walking onto the court in future matches.

Scores of course don't just stay in your memory, they can also be seen in print. A lot of clubs have a website giving information about their club and some have match and player results. Some leagues will also publish players' average scores at the end of the season. If the level of the league is high enough local newspapers might publish scores as well. This can be a motivation for winning by as positive a margin as you can or to get as many games in defeat as possible because if these scores are published they are there for all to see.

If you are a team captain why not ask your web designer to see if he can add a section where you and the other club captains can post your match scores. Individuals can sometimes be motivated when their scores are there for everyone to see so they become keener to win a set 6-0 rather than a relaxed 6-4, as it will look better.

Do you keep a diary? If you do and someone makes a compliment about part of your game then write it into your diary. When you look back at it in the future it will not just give you a lift but will often be representative of your key strength and therefore may remind you what to focus on in your matches.

So to create your confidence platform, look into your past and pick out one or two of your highlights. Think of scores or performances that made you proud. Do you have these in your head? If so you now have your confidence platform. This is the first layer. You are now going to build upon this.

STAGE 2 - FINDING THE OPPONENT'S WEAKNESS AND EXPLOITING IT

Let's assume you have played your opponent before and have built your confidence platform either from your last match against this opponent or from another match against a different opponent. This confidence platform might have been created on the basis that you won by a comprehensive margin last time or built on the fact that you only just lost by a narrow margin (because you scrapped for everything). You therefore have either a feeling of supreme confidence that you are stronger than your opponent or that you are within touching distance of beating him and feel you can do it this time. The next step is to believe that your opponent has a weakness and once you believe this, to find the weakness and exploit it.

Sometimes when you are playing against someone you feel is a lot stronger it can be hard to believe that he has any weaknesses. He does of course. The bottom line is that if the player had no weakness he would be playing at the top of the professional game and you know for a fact that the guy you are facing has not played at Wimbledon, therefore he has weaknesses. This is basic indisputable logic and should always be taken onto court with you. Your opponent has weaknesses. Fact. The question you set yourself before every match is therefore, "What is his key weakness".

The next step is finding the weakness. The most common weakness is the backhand. Opponents struggle particularly with high kicking topspins to the backhand so if you are able to play that shot then it is worth a try. Opponent's consistency can lessen also when playing shots on the run so moving him about by using angles and drop shots might be worth trying. These are two good examples of what is worth checking out early on with any opponent.

There are different ways of finding out the weaknesses of a specific individual and some were covered in the chapter on listening to your opponent. If you have played your opponent before then you should have learnt what his weaknesses are – there is no excuse for not having done this. McEnroe, in his book 'Serious' comments, "'one of my strengths had been the ability to figure out an opponent's game after I'd played him once". If you didn't gather this information then you need to work it out as quickly as possible and put it in the memory bank for future meetings. You might be in the fortunate position where you can sit on the sidelines and discretely watch the opponent first before you play him. There is also an opportunity in the warm up to assess any weaknesses although beware as knock ups are not always a good guide as a player might be hitting a slow forehand or backhand just to get it warmed up and also to bluff his opponent into thinking a particular shot is weak. There are numerous ways to find a player's weakness, indeed speaking to someone who knows the player's game is usually a good one.

You should be aware that a player can take time to get his shots warmed up and that what you perceive to be his weakness early on as you are winning point after point playing to it, may start to get grooved as it is getting so much practice. The good news here is that as he will have been playing that shot all the time then his other strokes will be getting rusty. Therefore as you are playing a match you should always be looking out for the situation of a player's weakness improving. If you are seeing this occur then you need to switch to playing away from this shot at the pivotal point, i.e. the point where he is winning as many shots as he is losing on it.

Once you change your target to be shots that he hasn't been using which would be the ones that you would normally consider to be his stronger ones then it is likely that you will be able to glean a few points that you wouldn't normally as he has not been playing the stroke as much. Before long though the advantage will reduce and again you should keep an eye out for the pivotal point, which will arrive sooner this time as you are playing to his strength, then switch back to his weakness. At this point your opponent may be grooved however you may well be ahead by a set just because of the tactics you have applied. If you able to find other weaknesses also such as lack of pace or poor volleying then move onto these as well.

Once you know the opponent's weaknesses – play on them!

A new layer has now been added as we build up our foundation using psychology and logic.

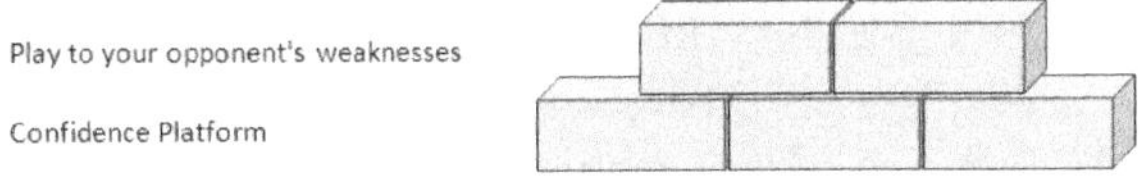

STAGE 3 - PLAYING TO YOUR STRENGTHS

Now you have the confidence you can win, the knowledge that your opponent has weaknesses and what those weaknesses are. You now need to apply a further piece of logic namely to play to your own strengths, i.e. playing your most successful stroke as often as you can and at the same time playing on your opponent's weakness as frequently as possible. You will no doubt be aware of your strongest stroke. When it is a key match or a key part of a match make sure you use it as much as possible. Save using your weaker shots for other less important matches or less crucial points in the match.

Our Psychological Foundation has now been built.

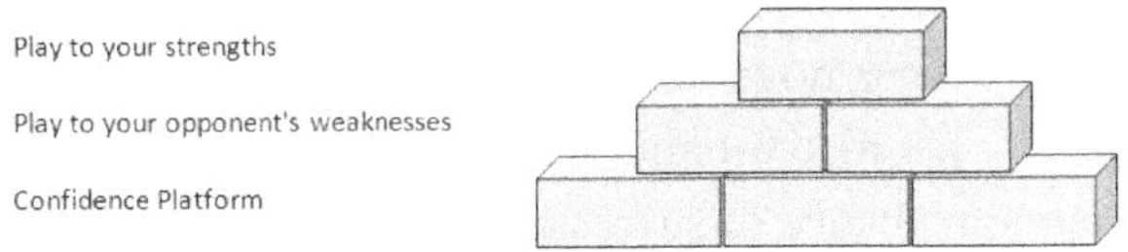

SECTION 2 – WINNING THE EXTRA POINT

If you adhere to the Psychological Foundation then you are now ready to consider the ways in which you can win that extra point. Below are a number of useful tips to do this.

TIPS ON BEING MATCH-TIGHT

In order to play a tennis match it is obvious to say that one or both of the players must keep score. A second reason for keeping score is to ensure you are not cheated out of points by your opponent. There is a third, more subtle reason though. Just as the hand-tap in doubles can be used to snap your concentration back to the next point, calling out the score can do the same. Instead of thinking about your kids, the crowd or what you need to get at the supermarket, your mind for the period when you are thinking about and calling out the score is a period where you are 100% concentrating on your tennis match, even if it is only for an instant. Keeping score every point therefore, whether you shout it out or not is a great form of concentration and must always be part of your game. The player who is forever asking the score is not concentrating hard enough on the match. This means if your opponent keeps asking the score it can be a good sign.

Let's focus now on the mentality you should have, i.e. how to be match-tight, in order to give yourself the maximum chance of success:-

1. Get ahead in the set.
2. Pretend you are a professional and adopt the mentality of the professional. Your job is to win the next point. After that point, whatever the result of the point just played, your job is to win the next point, then the next point, then the next

point, then the next point. I have repeated these words over and over but I do this for a reason. If you have won ten points in a row then your concentration should be just the same to win the eleventh as it was to win the first. This goal never changes, it is always the same. You will play no unprofessional shots.

3. Once you have the opponent where you want him, crush him. Don't let him up for air. Don't give him a line to let him haul himself back into the game. Give him nothing. Your aim should be for your opponent to believe that he has no chance of coming back into the match.
4. When you get to 5-0, 5-1 etc. then before the next game starts you say to yourself and to your partner, "We win this first time. We don't think to ourselves we have more chance of winning the game after this so we will let this one game go". You must go after every chance you have to win the set and you must make sure you do it as soon as possible.

In Tennis Psychology (Geist and Martinez) comment, "A universal axiom in tennis is to maintain as much pressure on your opponent as possible during every part of the match. The trick in this psychological

is to get on top and stay on top. One of the ways of maintaining pressure is to rush the net as much as possible".

At this point it is important to say that you should enjoy playing tennis but for a lot of people winning and enjoyment go hand in hand. The better your score the happier you are.

WINNING THE NEXT POINT

You will have heard the phrase 'Look after the pennies and the pounds will take care of themselves'. Similarly, in tennis, it is very much a case of 'Look after the points and the games will take care of themselves'.

A common thought in a player's mind is to look a game ahead and picture the score after winning the next game. The problem with this outlook, despite being positive, is that it relies too much on hope and not enough on concentration on the next shot. When Bjorn Borg was asked what was the most important reason for his incredibly successful tennis career, he replied, "It was my ability to play one point at a time and not worry and think about what just happened or what might happen".

When ahead in a set, a common fault of most players is to become complacent and think that losing a game or two at 5-1 up isn't a disaster. Over the course of your life if you are playing tennis regularly then it is highly likely that you are going to both win and lose sets from e.g. 5-0 or 5-1. The key is to try and achieve the seemingly impossible more times than being embarrassed and handing your opponent glory for years to come! The point being made here is the importance of concentrating on winning the next point. Make sure you inflict the psychological blow by coming back from 5-0 down rather than it being the other way round.

It is not only you that will remember a good score line you have achieved against an opponent, the opponent will as well. It is highly likely you will have to play the opponent many times again – probably twice a year if you are a regular match player.

Let's look at a particular scenario. You play an opponent who is a similar standard to you and you have an extremely close set and win 6-4. Let's say your opponent loses heart just a little in the second set because of the first set loss and despite being fairly close again, you win the second set 6-2. The match might have been extremely close but you have come out of it with a 6-4, 6-2 win. If someone else sees this on paper they will think it was a routine win and may tell others or compliment you thus boosting your confidence. When your opponent remembers back he will remember the score and it puts doubts in his mind for the next time. This is the importance of keeping your foot pressed hard down on your opponent and not letting him escape.

Tennis players often use physical actions to improve psychological performance for example doing something to bring concentration round to the next point. Britain's Tim Henman explained that he used the time when he was bouncing the ball prior to serving to decide where he was going to place the next serve and how he was going to play the next point. All players bounce the ball but do you do this because you are using this time to plan your next move or are you just copying what you see everyone else doing and bouncing a ball a few times before you serve? Such physical actions are also a way of taking your mind off any nerves you might be suffering. French player Marianne Bartoli hops up and down before points as her way of getting ready for the next point. So from this we can see that physical methods can have a positive psychological effect.

The key to winning every point is to maximise and

maintain your concentration levels throughout the match and reduce the number of times you switch off. This is something you can work at improving until you get to a professional level of concentration. Maureen Connelly once said, "You could set off dynamite on the next court and I wouldn't notice". That's the level you need to aim to get to. You may not be able to get to a professional level at playing tennis but you can certainly achieve it at a psychological level.

Oddly the formatting in the way matches are played, as decreed by leagues rules, can have an effect on your concentration levels. If a normal set is nearing its conclusion and it's on a knife's edge then it is fascinating to see who cracks or who takes control. However in the earlier games in the set there might not be the same mental challenge especially if a player is leading by quite a margin. Other possible formats consist of playing a set number of games, twelve for example, against each opposing pair and the teams' total number of games are totted up at the end of the match. The key to success in this latter format is total concentration throughout the 'set' of twelve games rather than the peaks and troughs mindset of standard sets. It can take months and in most cases a small number of years for players to train themselves to concentrate fully in every point of every game of a match but interestingly it's this different format where every game counts that can help improve your concentration levels during a match so that you are fighting for every point.

If you find that at less stressful points in a set, such as 1-1 in the first set, you are lacking the intensity you might feel if it was 5-6 30-40, convince yourself that the score is actually set point and think about the feelings that you usually have at that point. Project those onto the present and you should be able to significantly increase your motivation to win the next point.

So it can be seen that there are physical and psychological ways of improving your chances of winning the next point.

SNAP THE FOCUS BACK

The fundamental theme running through this book is that of concentrating on the next point and in the few books that are available in relation to tennis psychology some of them focus on the four C's. For completeness we include these here:-

Concentration,
Confidence,
Commitment,
Calm/Control

Some books also include a fifth element of 'Refocusing after errors'.

These elements are excellent in theory, however when you are in the heat of a match that is important to you then it is likely that one element, commitment, will be high and another element, confidence, will take care of itself if you start winning more points than you are losing. This leaves concentration, control/calm and refocusing after errors. In essence these can all be addressed using the same technique namely employing a trigger to refocus your concentration before each point.

Techniques for focusing include using a trigger phrase that you think up that works for you. That phrase for example could be 'low slice backhand' to remind you of the shot your opponent does not like. Another trigger phrase might be 'fight like Nadal'. By doing this your concentration is on the next point, you are instilling calm by having a game plan or more accurately a shot-plan and therefore you feel more in control. So by saying one phrase you can achieve all the key elements without having to think about them individually.

A common occurrence in tennis is when one player has won the first set by a comfortable margin he then gives away the first game in the second set really easily. You will often see a score line mid-way through a match of 6-0, 0-1. Even if the player who has won the first set forces himself to concentrate and fight for the first game of the second set it can still be a surprisingly difficult game to win. The reason for this is down to human nature. One player has built a plateau for himself, namely the winning of the first set, and therefore the instinctive mental reaction is to rest. This occurs at the same point in time as the opponent who has been behind for quite a time suddenly finds himself level at 0-0 at the start of the new set and has a fresh start.

So the next time you have won the first set of a match 6-0, then the first game in the second set should be worthy of increased attention on your part, so set yourself the challenge of winning it. Not just to hammer another nail in your opponent's coffin but also to see if you can achieve the mental challenge of winning this particular game.

THE FIRST TWO POINTS OF THE GAME

One of the most successful techniques I have adopted is saying to my partner that in each game our aim is to be 30-0 up and that our worst case scenario is to be 15-15. The aim is to try at the start of each game to get to the same level of concentration that you have if the score was game point. The start of each game is undoubtedly a subconscious lull time for both sides as the mind naturally defaults to thinking it can afford to drop a point or two and still recover to win the game or that a player's serve will bail them out. This means there is a great opportunity for you to get an advantage at the start of a game. If you get to 30-0 you are 50% of the way to winning the game of course.

MIMIC THE PROFESSIONAL

Pretend you are a professional and that you have now adopted the mentality of the professional on the tour. To be the best they eat correctly, train correctly, warm up and warm down correctly, are desperate to win and fight for every point. Train yourself to have the same mentality, you will soon enjoy thinking professionally and will be able to add another psychological string to your bow by knowing that the player you are facing cannot be any more prepared than you and most likely will not be as prepared.

FIGHTING FOR THAT NEXT COMPLIMENT

Another reason to battle for every game and to get as

good a score as you can and play as well as you can, is to receive a compliment. The compliment can come from various sources such as from your own team, a spectator or the opposition. Whoever it is from it is a great feeling to receive one especially as they are not banded about too freely. Once you have had one you will want another and another and another.

Compliments can be about a number of topics, for example about the good behaviour of a young player after he has lost or a player who just runs and runs for everything and never gives up or just the fact that a player is a good player and has won yet again. Regardless of how you get the compliment it can become like a drug that is craved and you will certainly get more if you cover all your bases such as having a good temperament, fighting for every point etc.

NEVER GIVE UP

There will be matches where you realise that your opponent is comprehensively stronger than you. You should never give up the fight though as you never know what might happen. An opponent may often have peaks and troughs in his game even just over the course of one set. Also any player can be subject to an injury at any time and may be unable to continue. The bottom line is that if you are still in the match then you can still win it. One of the bonuses of tennis as opposed to football and rugby is that if you are losing you are not under time pressure to come back and win – just regular pressure!

Even if your opponent is significantly stronger try

keeping him on court just to see if he tires. If it's a doubles team match and you are sending your opponents scurrying around the court then although you and your partner may not benefit from your opponents' tiring legs in the set you are playing against them, assuming they have two more rounds to play against your team-mates then the team as a whole may well reap the benefits as the match goes on due to the pair you are playing expending so much energy early on against you and your partner.

MAKING YOUR OPPONENTS LOOK AND FEEL BAD

All the points made above are to encourage you to win as many points as possible and get as good a score as you can. You will find that if you thrash players, particularly if it is 6-0, 6-0 it will stay with them as long as they live. It will also appear in their mind every time they play you in the future. Margaret Thatcher once spoke of dictators, that it wasn't enough to destroy their armies and just beat them, they must be humiliated in front of their own people. Okay this sounds a bit heavy for a tennis court but if you can adopt the 'destroying the opponent' mentality on the tennis court as your starting point and assuming you don't quite achieve this level you will still be of the mindset of wiping your opponent off the court, which is a good mindset to have. If you do thrash a player though ensure you show some modesty. As football pundit Glenn Hoddle once said, "Arrogance has a habit of turning around and slapping you in the face".

SUMMARY

Adopt the following in order to help you win that extra point:-

- Keep match tight i.e. maximum concentration
- Don't let your opponent up for air if you have him where you want him
- Pretend you are on the professional circuit and adopt the same attitude
- Physical actions can enhance psychological performance
- If you have just won a set then challenge yourself to win the first game in the next set
- Set a two point target in each game so that you are aiming to be winning 30-0 in each game
- Try to elicit compliments from people to further enhance your confidence
- Never give up

If you have the chance to inflict a damaging score line on your opponent; do it.

5 SHOTS TO PLAY AND MOVEMENTS TO MAKE

BASIC DOUBLES LOGIC

Allen Fox, Brad Gilbert's former coach, provides the mathematical logic for the correct doubles strategy, "Much doubles strategy is a natural consequence of the fact that each partner of a doubles team is responsible for substantially less territory than singles. In singles one player has to cover the entire width of the court which is twenty-seven feet. In doubles there is an additional player but the court is widened by only nine feet, leaving each player responsible for only eighteen feet. The major fallout from this fact is that attacking at the net becomes more profitable in doubles rather than singles. So the first general rule in doubles is that the team at the net has the advantage. Serving is more of an advantage in doubles than singles because it allows the serving team the first opportunity to advance both players into the volley position. This gives them control of the net and a high probability of winning the point."

Fox also advises on serve, "Where should you serve in doubles? On a strictly geometric basis the best place to serve is down the middle. From this position it is difficult for the receiver to hit down the line and pass the partner stationed at the net. It also reduces the angle for the return intended to pass the server who is moving forward. Finally it enables the server's partner to poach more easily as there is less concern with the down-the-line return."

PREDICTING YOUR OPPONENTS NEXT SHOT

If you are playing against weak players it is worth watching out for the player who will return across court, shot after shot regardless. This is the player who will continue to hit the ball across court despite his opponent at the net moving across and intercepting each shot. In doing this the net player is leaving a yawning gap down his line but the returner does not appear to be able to see the obvious space to hit into or presumably believes himself unable to adjust his body to hit the ball down the line. If you are the net player and have found that in a game you are facing a player who is seemingly unable to hit anywhere other than across court then you can just pick off return after return. Don't be afraid to keep poaching your partner's shots even if at times your line feels uncomfortably exposed.

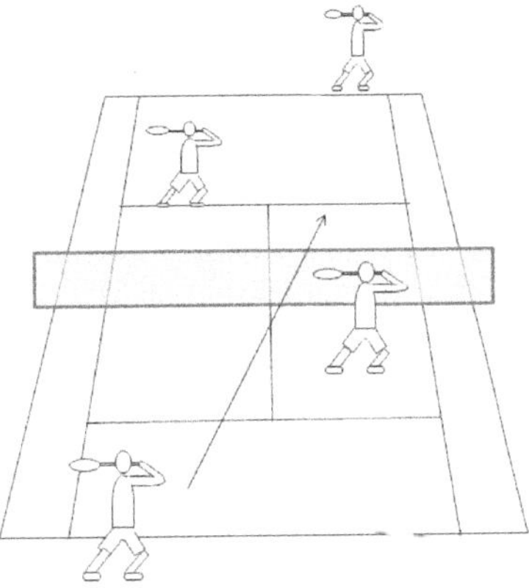

Fig 1 The basic player may only ever return across court

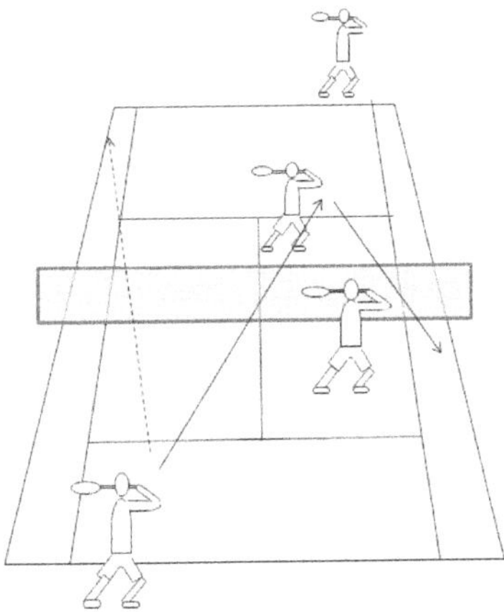

Fig 2 The net player will just keep intercepting. The dashed arrow shows the obvious shot to play

Although this may seem very obvious, I am

highlighting it to make a point to many players. It is amazing the number of players who either don't spot this pattern or do spot it but fail to act on it. If you are one of these players then look for it and when the occasion arises – step out of your comfort zone and get poaching!

It is quite rare to come across a player who never hits down an open tramline, however many are not comfortable doing it. So in most cases in order to tell where a player is going to hit a shot you need to draw on a number of things. One is experience and the other is from the opponent's body language. Below are some practical examples of this. Use/Consider the following:-

- Your experience of where your opponent would normally aim the next shot given the position he is in when he is about to hit the ball
- Your experience of where this particular opponent usually hits his shots e.g. in doubles he might be obsessed with trying to return down the net player's tram line
- Your own movement, i.e. if you are at the net and have crossed over on the previous two occasions, then by dummying to move again but actually staying where you are, can force your opponent to occasionally hit the ball where you want him to hit it, i.e. straight to you.
- Whether he is angry with you and you think he is going to aim the ball at your head!
- His stance added to your knowledge of whether your opponent could pull out an unexpected angle from how he is standing

As you play better players it becomes a little harder to predict what they are going to do but still always study your opponent continually to increase the accuracy of your predictions.

THE NET MANIAC

In doubles one of the most satisfying things when you are playing at the net is when your opponent dumps his return in the bottom of the net purely through your movement at the net. To win a point by not actually playing a shot is extremely useful as not only is it another way to win a point but is a lot less risky than going for a winner and a lot less tiring than rallying for ten shots until your opponent makes a mistake. It gives you an uplifting feeling and not only does it depress your opponent but it can also give him doubt and concern for the next point and often for many after that.

It is possible to see quite easily how your opponent deals with being put under pressure by just watching his facial expression around the time he is hitting the ball and immediately after he has guided the ball out of the court in order to avoid you at the net. It's often the case that he will tell you that he is struggling by complaining that he missed the shot because of you moving at the net. This is music to the ears.

The best way to understand the effect of a net player's movement is to face someone in a doubles match who poaches and causes havoc at the net and remember what you are thinking at the time, how you feel playing against him and the problems that he is causing you.

Having played against players such as this though, as you no doubt will have done at some point, it is now your aim to inflict the psychological issues you had dealing with it, onto others. Whereas you may have only faced one or two players who cause havoc at the net, you should be aiming to cause problems to everyone you play against.

Whilst commentating on a mixed match in Australia, Martina Navratilova advised, "The guy's job at the net is to get into the head of the woman particularly".

In doubles, if you find yourself playing against a player who is dominating the net successfully and is all over your partner's returns, then there is often only one way to solve the problem. If you are a good volleyer then do the same and make sure you start causing more damage to his partner then he is causing to yours. Sometimes, even though you might feel teamwork and a partnership is about taking an equal number of shots, if you are stronger than your partner, then often you have to take control of the match and take more than your share.

Navratilova comments, "In doubles you have to own the middle of the net, whoever does, wins".

Allen Fox comments, "There is nothing more soothing to a receiving team than to know that the server's partner will not poach. The receiver knows exactly where to hit every time. Instead, make him worry. Move around. Force him to make a split-second decision on each return as to whether to hit crosscourt or down the line. He will never get into a comfortable groove".

It is also worth being aware that the stage the game is at can make a difference to the effectiveness of the net player. Fox discusses arousal levels in players, "Pressure raises an opponent's level of arousal. At an early stage of a match, say 2-all in the first set, the arousal level may be low and attacking the net may excite the baseliner just enough to stimulate some good passing shots. However, at 5-all in the third set, when he is under great pressure to begin with, a net attack can raise the baseliner's level of arousal to such uncomfortable heights that hitting a successful passing shot becomes very difficult. Brad Gilbert found that passing shots which were routine early in the match became hard in the late stages. He learned to come to the net himself on the big points so the other guy could choke first."

THE PAWN SACRIFICE

Here we compare tennis with chess. One of the best things to try the first time you are at the net and your partner is serving is to launch yourself across the net to try and pick off your opponent's return. The first return an opponent makes in a match is virtually guaranteed to be returned back across court. The reason for this is that the cross court return is the usual shot of most players and is therefore the default when they are not quite awake yet. Also they want to play safe early on because they are unlikely to have their returns grooved to the point that they feel confident enough to hit a winner down your tramline this early in the match. If you are the net player this gives you a great window of opportunity.

The reason that this is called the pawn sacrifice is

because even if you lose the point (sacrificing your pawn) it is fairly likely you will gain overall on the next few points (future moves). Don't underestimate the power of the unsuccessful poach. Regardless of whether you are successful or not on the first point, why not try the same again the next time the same opponent returns. On the third return though it's probably best to stay put. It does depend how your opponent is coping with it though – keep watching him for signs. If you have stayed where you are on the third return then why not try the poach again on the fourth return. Also consider how your partner is feeling as he may not be keen on you poaching too much.

So let's apply this theory to a mixed match where we move through it one point at a time and explain the thought process of the opponent who is facing the net player who poaches. The theory we are going to try is illustrated here, namely:-

1. Poach opposition lady's first return
2. Poach opposition lady's second return
3. Stay put for the opposition lady's third return
4. Poach opposition lady's fourth return

So the first game begins:-

Score 0-0

The players are shown in Fig 3. The man at the bottom of the illustration (pl 1) is serving to the lady (pl 4) at the top. The server's partner at the net (pl 2) has decided that on the first point she is going to intercept the lady's return (pl 4) whatever return shot is played, as shown. In this example, the lady (pl 4) receiving the serve does not expect the interception and dumps the return into the net due to the sudden movement of the net player (pl 2).

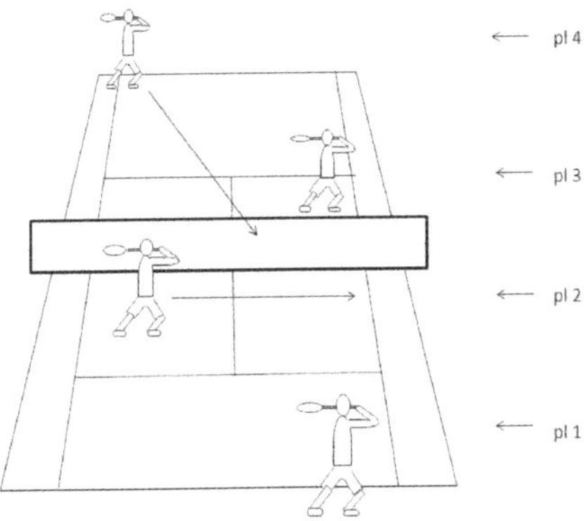

Fig 3 The effect of poaching on the first point

Score: 15-0

The server (pl 1) now serves to the man (pl 3). The server's partner (pl 2) at the net decides that she is going to stay where she is. In this particular game the server loses the point this time.

Score: 15-15

The server (pl 1) serves to the lady (pl 4) again. The server's partner at the net (pl 2) decides that she is again going to intercept the ladies return whatever shot is played. The lady receiving the serve does not expect the net opponent to poach a second time in succession. This time she gets the return back in court however the net player volleys the ball away for a winner.

Score: 30-15

The server (pl 1) serves to the man (pl 3) for the second time. Again the server's partner at the net stays where she is as it is not in her plan to poach against the man. The pair serving end up winning the point this time.

Score: 40-15

The server serves to the lady again. Having poached twice in a row on this side the server's partner at the net decides to stay where she is, as per the plan. She is thinking through the thought process that would logically be taking place in the mind of the lady receiving. The lady receiving is highly likely to now think that her opponent at the net is likely to poach every time and also wants to teach her a lesson namely to stay in her tramline. The lady receiving therefore hits her return down the tramline instead of across court. The lady at the net who has stayed where she is just volleys the ball away for a winner.

Score: Game.

This game was essentially split into two parts. When the server serves to the lady who is receiving in the deuce court then the theory is applied. When the server serves to the gentleman in the advantage court then it is not applied and the server's partner stays where she is. In this game there were only three points played to the lady in the deuce court therefore all four parts of the theory were not tested, only the first three. It does enough though for you to see the pattern being applied and therefore for you to replicate it on court.

Essentially here we are planting seeds of doubt in the opponent's mind and you can gain a great many points from this. Particularly look out for players' weaknesses. If the opponent is weaker on his backhand side then get your partner to serve to his backhand and keep intercepting.

It is common to find younger players continuing to hit their returns across court as they have often come from playing a lot of singles rather than doubles and are just not used to the idea of hitting to a place where someone is stood at the time of playing the shot. Older players too who have played the same shots for decades can be so set in their ways they won't feel confident enough to change their grooved shots. Then there are other players who perhaps aren't physically comfortable with adjusting their body to play shots down the line.

As the match progresses it is likely that you probably won't be able to poach quite as much however it will undoubtedly have got you off to a good start. In a close game of doubles, more often than not the pair who win are the pairing who have the strongest net player.

PAWN SACRIFICE – REVERSING THE LOGIC

If you are receiving serve at the start of a match and you know your opponent at the net is going to poach or if you have played a few points and have worked out that the net player is regularly leaving his tramline open, then hit the return down his tramline early on in the match and, if needs be, at regular intervals thereafter.

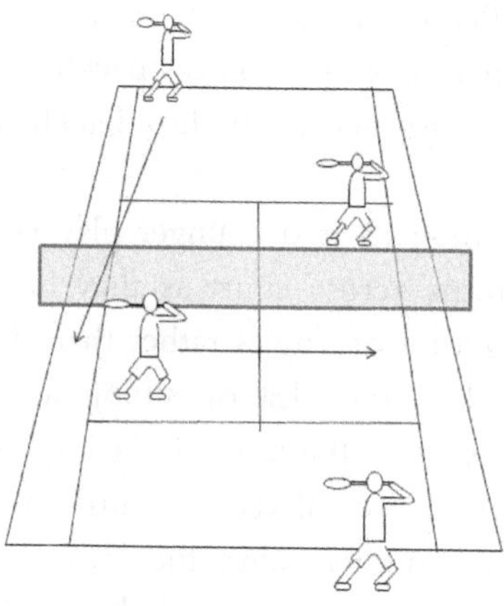

Fig 4 Striking the ball down your opponent's line

This is a much underused weapon particularly in lower league tennis. Hitting down the opponent's line may give you a winner either because he has moved out of position or because he is still standing there and is not expecting the ball to come straight at him so can't react in time to get it back.

Even if it doesn't get you a winner and even if the

opponent just stands there and punches the volley away you will still make greater gains in the coming points. This is because your opponent will have doubts in his mind about leaving his tramline unprotected so will not poach as much. So in essence you have sacrificed one point to gain others later on, hence the pawn sacrifice analogy.

N.H.Patterson in 'Lawn Tennis Courtcraft' states "In teaching a game like lawn tennis one must of course teach orthodox strokes and tactics first – the basis of the game. But I want to suggest to you that most of you, not perhaps beginners, but those who would be placed in the first class of a handicap event, are very much too orthodox. You do not mix your game up half enough, and your play and tactics lack that important element – surprise".

PLAYING CHESS WITH YOUR OPPONENT

If you are considerably stronger than the player you are playing against then how about working at developing your touch play and control by trying to toy with your opponent and tire him out. You might for example try drop shotting him, then when he reaches the ball and scoops it back up to you, lob him, etc. Try working at your placement of the ball and attempting more acute angles to your shots. Another way to look at this is that you are moving your opponent around the court as though it was a chessboard, dictating where you want him to go.

Moving away from toying with the opposition and

more towards concentrating on winning the point, we come back to another similarity to chess. Assuming you are not in a position where you can hit an outright winner then your aim is to be in a stronger position after your next shot then you are at present i.e. you are setting up the winner which you are hoping to clinch in the next shot (or the one after). Essentially a building process. So you play a shot to move your opponent into a position you want him to be in, so you can win the game on the next shot. In chess terms you might move him to a particular spot by sacrificing a small piece, in order to benefit on your next move by getting checkmate having moved him out of position in the previous move.

So the net player hits the ball into the space (arrowed below in Fig 5) to move his opponent there, building the point:-

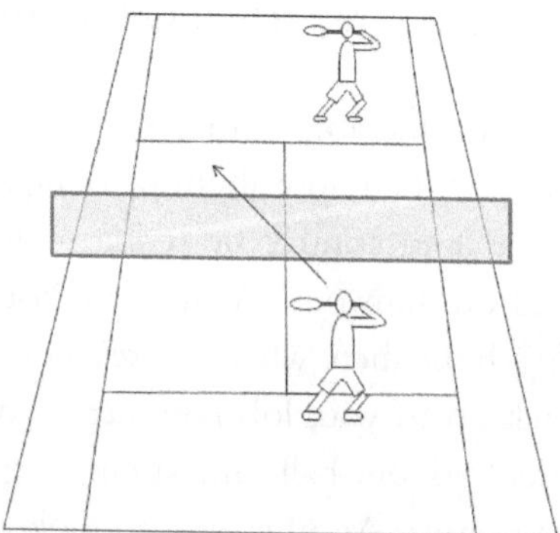

Fig 5 Drop shot played into the space to make the opponent move. The head of the arrow is where the ball lands

The opponent gets to the ball but can only scoop it up to the net player who then wins the shot (Fig 6):-

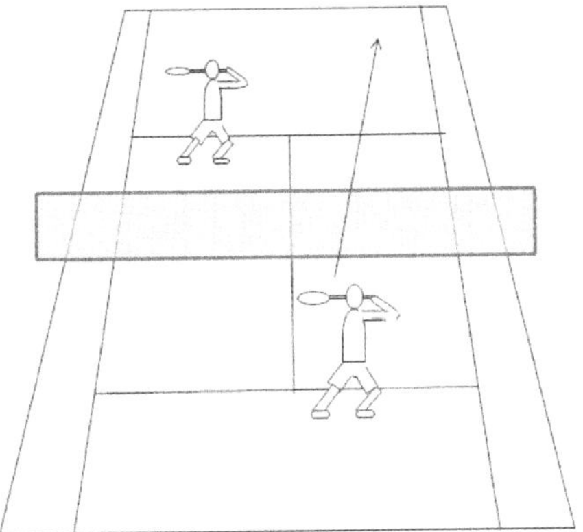

Fig 6 Finishing the point

On the chess board, white moves his pawn to the square it can be seen in below, tempting black to move his bishop to take it (Fig 7):-

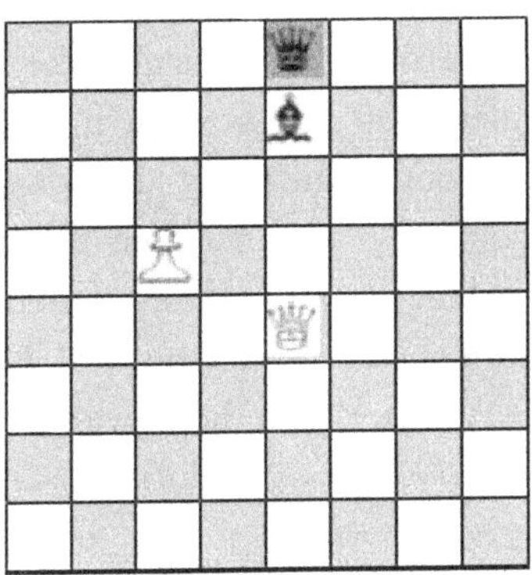

Fig 7 White sacrifices his pawn

Black gains a pawn but loses out (Fig 8):-

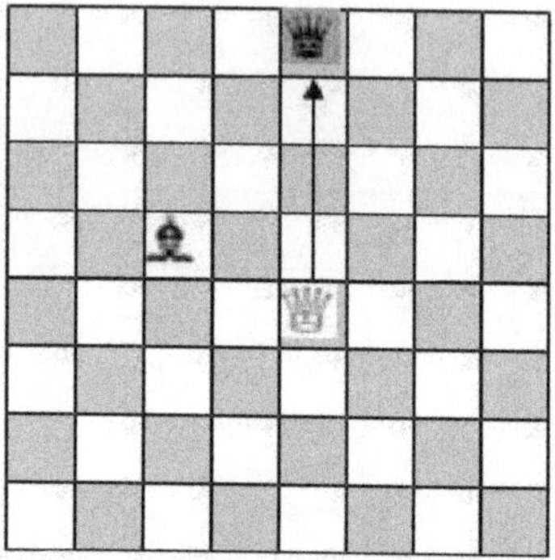

Fig 8 White queen takes the black queen, thus winning this contest

ANGLES

One of the wonderful elements of racket sports is the geometrical side of it, in particular the angle that it is possible to play shots and how far it is possible to send your opponent out of the court. It is obvious to say that the nearer you are to the net then the better the angle that can be achieved. If you are partnering a big server then this means your opponent will have a problem lobbing the ball over your head with his return as the stronger the serve the more difficult it is to control an accurate lob return which means that you are able to stand pretty much on top of the net. Although when you are first being taught to play tennis you will be told of the correct distance to stand from the net, once you become a little more experienced then try stepping in to the point where it may feel uncomfortable and if you can intercept a return use such an acute angle that it is impossible for your opponent to return the ball. Your aim should be to play the ball at such an angle that the people on the adjacent court have to stop their game due to your ball ending up in the middle of their court or alternatively if you are playing on the end court, that you send your opponent crashing into the perimeter side fencing! If you find players are beginning to describe you as a geometric sadist, then try to take this as a compliment, as it means its working.

Often on indoor courts you will have the netting drawn alongside each court to divide the courts. Logic dictates that when serving if you are able to serve the ball as near to the tramlines as possible then you will have a good chance of curling the ball into the divide netting and getting a free point. Try taking speed off the serve as well as playing the angle and you will find you have a very effective serve. This means that instead of the receiver having to move sideways across the court he also has to move forwards therefore having to cover a larger distance. This will take a split second longer which will be sufficient to get the ball to hit the side netting first. Consider the geometrical logic below.

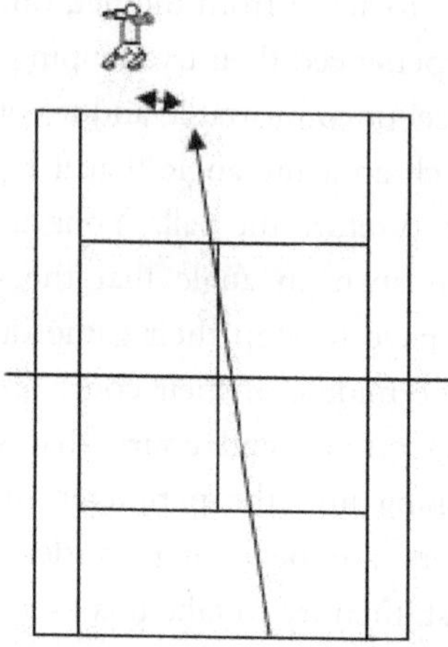

Fig 9 The receiver has only to move a couple of metres in order to play the shot.

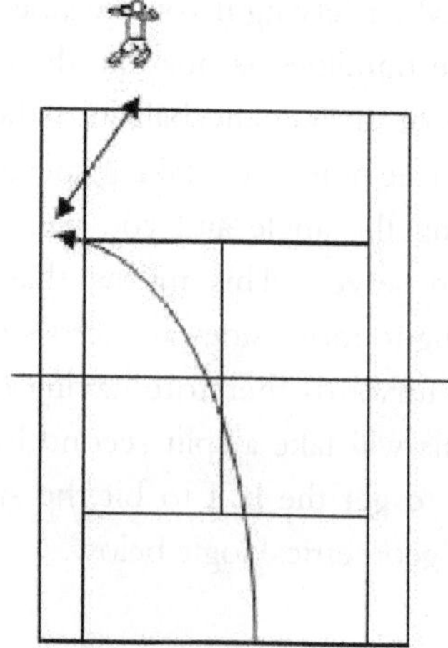

Fig 10 In the above example, the receiver has to move considerably further in order to return the slower serve.

Sometimes brain can be more effective than brawn. Power and speed are not everything in tennis.

In John McEnroe's autobiography 'Serious' he comments, "I began to look at the court differently – as a mathematical equation almost. The angles were everything. It wasn't about just hitting a slice and approaching the net. Sometimes you should slice it deep, but sometimes you could come in and slice it off the court – *use the angle*"

DROP-SHOTTING THE ELDERLY

There are only two moral rules I believe everyone should have on a tennis court, firstly that you shouldn't cheat and secondly that the gentleman should not smash the ball deliberately at the lady in mixed doubles. My view is that everything else is fair game.

One of the moral questions you might ask yourself is whether winning lots of points against your opponents by drop shotting the seventy five year old who is playing against you, who clearly can't get to the ball, is ethically correct. My personal opinion is that I wouldn't do it during club play with fellow club members as essentially people are coming down to the club to have a hit and don't want to be humiliated.

Match play is a little different and I believe that anything (other than the above two rules) goes. The reason for this is that the elderly opponent has decided to put himself into the situation of a match and is therefore doing everything he can to win, exactly the same as you. Also look upon it as a challenge for your opponents.

Often an older player will be playing with someone who has a lot greater movement. The quicker player will usually work out pretty swiftly that you are intending to drop shot his elderly partner and so needs to come up with a plan to counter it which is usually sprinting over and getting to the drop shot. This will naturally leave a large space in the rest of the court for you or your partner to put the opponents return into. It is your opponents' choice at that point whether the older player covers the space that his partner, who has retrieved the drop shot, has left behind. So view this as not a case of you being cruel but more a case of you presenting a challenge to your opponents to come up with a solution between them in order to stop you hitting anymore drop shots. Remember you are not just playing against the elderly player; you are playing against two players. When the older player complains to you about you drop shotting him then he is saying these words in order to gain an advantage by making you feel guilty about playing a perfectly legal shot.

If on the other hand you are the elderly person in question we have just talked about, then you probably don't need any advice as you are playing the best psychological game you can when you make your complaint to your opponent – making him feel guilty is an excellent way of suppressing the variety of his shots. As the tongue in cheek saying goes 'Age and treachery will always overcome youth and skill'.

TOYING WITH THE SERVER'S MIND

When playing doubles, servers can often be put off by the opponent at the net. There are a couple of ways the server can be put off, firstly by any movement of the net player at the point he is serving (it is entirely legal to jump around like a madman but I'm not about to start recommending it) or secondly by the position that the net player has taken up (a great way of causing psychological problems for the server). If the net player on the receiving side is stood so far across that he is almost standing in his partner's service box then it can be quite off putting. An example is shown in fig 11 with the net player highlighted and the arrow showing where the server is trying to server.

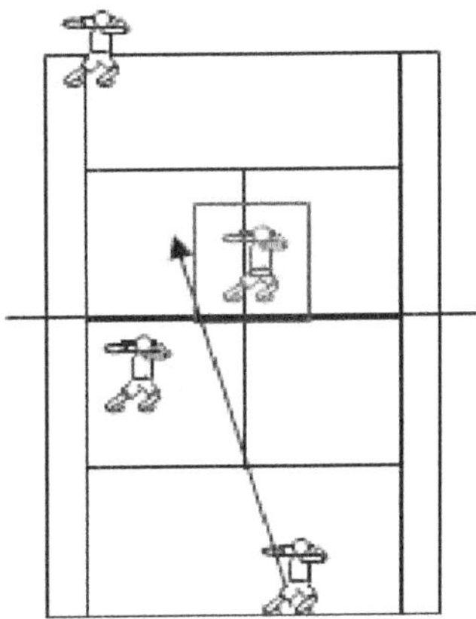

Fig 11 Toying with the server's mind

This standing position for the receiving net player is usually only recommended against a player's second serve. This is due to two reasons, firstly you are liable to get hit if you are stood there for a first serve and secondly there is considerably more pressure on the server when he is hitting a second serve as opposed to a first serve which at local club level is pretty much a shot to nothing. It is sensible to stand across on the opponent's serve only at key times otherwise if you do it regularly then he will get accustomed to it and the effect of your standing position will diminish. It is recommended for the net player to stand in an off putting position on the server's second serve on breakpoint. Make sure that if it is your partner and not you at the net he does the same. If you have elected to use this tactic on something other than breakpoint and the server has clearly been affected and has served a double fault then make a visible point of going over to your partner and speaking to him and asking him to do the same on the next point i.e. stand across at the net. The server who is feeling pretty bad about it now feels a whole lot worse as he knows his psychological flaws are being discussed as well.

Two things to consider though are firstly whether by standing in an unusual position you are not putting your partner off more than the server. It is worth asking your partner before you play with him for the first time whether he minds you standing so far over and tell him the reason why you are doing it. The other thing to consider is that if you do this to your opponent then it is virtually a guarantee that he will do the same back to you when you are serving. However, because of his anger and keenness to get revenge (or to show that he thinks about the psychology of the game as well), he will often try this out against you straight away. However as doing this straight away will mean it is at the start of the next game it will usually be on a non critical point such as your first serve at the start of your service game. You can therefore continue the tactic as you are still getting an advantage over your opponents as you are applying it at the critical points which they probably won't realise. In trying to get revenge the opponent will have stepped out of his comfort zone as he is not used to standing so far across. He will be keen to get back into that comfort zone as soon as possible so having done it once just to make a point he will probably not continue to do it again in your service game as he will feel that he has had his say in return.

THE MATHEMATICAL POACHER

If you are the stronger player of your partnership then it is not unreasonable to take a slightly higher percentage of shots than your partner because logically as a partnership you will get better results that way. On the flip side if you poach too much and leave the court exposed then you are going to start losing points and demotivate your partner fairly quickly as well.

Consider the following mathematical model (you will need maximum concentration!):-

1. In the first four games of a match the leader in the partnership takes only a standard share of the shots, i.e. 50% and he notes the number of games won and lost.

2. In the next four games he takes 75% of the shots and notes the number of games won and lost.
3. Finally in the next four games he returns to a more normal proportion of 60% and keeps a tally there as well.

Let's assume we have the perfect model i.e. that all the players play at the same standard throughout the match and that the percentages above are pretty much on the mark. With these results the leader can then assess the proportion of the shots that he should take in order to optimise the results of the partnership. For example, when the player took 50% of the shots, they only won half the points, when he took 60% of the shots they won two thirds of the points but when he took 75% of the shots he was leaving too much of his own court open and the win percentage went back down to just half the points. The optimum in this example therefore was 60%.

Now this model clearly has flaws and assumptions but the reason for showing this example is to make it easier to map this blueprint into your mind as you play. If you are able to keep a mental log of how the match score changes depending upon how much you poach then you can optimise yours and your partner's results. Clearly there are many variables involved and this mental logging is not going to be in the forefront of your mind during a match. However at certain points during the match if you step back and think about the success or otherwise of a change to the percentage of shots you poach, then this will tell you whether you are taking too many or too few shots.

PUTTING PRESSURE ON THE SERVER

Have you ever tried standing closer in when receiving a serve to the point of standing almost on the service line? If you feel you have quick enough reactions then try standing just one metre behind the service line and seeing if you can get the opponent's serve back. I would recommend trying this in practice a few times rather than doing it straight away in a match.

So why do this? Well, it is to see if you can get a competitive advantage during a match using the element of surprise. Let us assume you have had a few goes in practice at trying to return serves when you are standing so close in and even when your opponent has hit a hard serve you have found that you have quick enough reactions to half volley the return back into court. We need to consider the advantages and disadvantages of this idea. These will become easier to remember if you try it yourself.

Disadvantages:-

- Offending your opponent. Standing so close in on a person's serve is a real snub to his ego and an opponent will undoubtedly get offended so try not to do it too often.
- Low percentage shot. The time you have to react is much less as you are standing closer in so it obviously increases the likelihood of the serve being successful.
- Lack of control of your return. As you are half volleying a fast serve you would be blocking the

ball back as your main aim is to get the ball back into play. This means that you will be sacrificing accuracy and placement so the ball will often sit up mid court for the server to take a swing at it on the next shot.

Advantages:-

- Psyching out your opponent. If you have a weak-minded opponent and the fact that you are standing so far in is seen as an attacking and arrogant intention then you could intimidate your opponent which could have a benefit as the match goes on.
- Element of surprise. It is unlikely that an opponent who believes himself to have a reasonable serve will ever have faced someone standing so far in, even having played for many years. It will undoubtedly throw the server a little.
- Lesser time needed to get into the net. Clearly as you have only half the distance to travel to get to the net you can get there sooner thus avoiding any potentially difficult half volleys during the rally.
- Ownership of the net. It encourages you to move forward into the net which is always where you should be aiming to be in doubles.
- Winning cheap points due to your opponent over compensating. In order to prove to you that you are wrong to stand so far in on a player's serve the server will often try to hit the serve harder and may even do two first serves in order to make a point. What often results from this is that the opponent actually loses the point as it increases his chance of doing a double fault.

The key to this encroaching tactic however is the obvious one, namely that it is used only very occasionally and must be done at the crucial time for example if your opponent is serving and is trailing 30-40 in the game so he is under maximum pressure.

HOW YOU HOLD YOUR RACKET

During matches I often decide to practice one particular shot and on one occasion when I was playing I wanted to work at improving my backhand topspin return. I was intending to work on the blocked topspin return on the opponent's faster first serve and then taking a swing at his second serve. After the match my opponent said to me that it had surprised him that I had been trying to return using backhands rather than forehands as usually players did the exact opposite. I was quite impressed by him noticing that I had been trying to return using my backhand as I hadn't particularly run around my forehand and as my return consistency wasn't much different on each wing then he had done well to pick up on this. I asked him how he noticed this and he pointed out a very obvious fact that was a subconscious trait that I had been doing without realising. We are all normally taught as kids to get in 'the ready position' where the racket head is pointed in the direction the ball is approaching from. In my plan to receive on my backhand side however I had my racket head pointed to the left so it gave me a split second more time as it was ready to receive a backhand. My opponent had noticed this and was sensibly therefore trying to serve to my forehand.

So this example re-iterates the importance of the correct readiness position but also highlights how when an opponent tells you something it is worth listening as it may help you in the future.

Turning this around the other way, it is worth you watching your opponent as you are about to serve to him to see if he has his racket positioned to accept either a forehand or backhand, as you can then serve to the opposite side to which he is prepared for, or indeed a hard body serve.

VOLLEYING IN DOUBLES

In 'Think To Win' Allen Fox advises, "If your team is serving, where should you hit your volleys? Normally, aim the first one down the middle of the court as deep as possible. Attempting an angle on the first volley is difficult because the server is not yet close enough to the net to have the wide angles open. If you try to hit an angle, it is unlikely to be severe enough to cause the defenders great difficulty. But on the negative side of the ledger, it will create openings along a sideline through which the defenders can hit drives. If both defenders are on the baseline, you should also direct subsequent volleys down the middle and deep unless there is an obvious opening. Hitting down the middle pulls both defenders to the centre of the court and produces openings in the areas they have been forced to abandon. If the receivers leave a man at the net and one on the baseline, work the ball as suggested earlier - hit tough volleys back deep to the baseline and easy ones at the net person.

If all four players are at the net, the team that gets closest to the net soonest will usually win the point. If you must hit a low volley, hit it back soft and low and move forward quickly. If you get a high volley, charge in and try to get on top of the net. Then smack it at or between your opponents. The key in these exchanges is to be mobile forward. Many players make the mistake of standing still on high volleys and taking a long swing at the ball. Only from close in can you consistently put the ball away."

PRACTISING RECEIVING SERVE

During the warm up against your opponents the obvious tip is to ensure you practice serving from both the deuce and advantage side. However try to ensure you also practice returning the opponent's service during the warm up. This is crucial to starting off well and to adjusting to the pace of the opponent's serve because often an opponent's serve is a lot faster pace than his normal ground strokes that you have been hitting against. Make sure as well as getting at least five of your own serves in at each side, that you also hit five returns in too. In doubles it is often difficult in a warm up to work it so that you get to practice returning each of your opponent's serves however you should aim to try and do this.

EXPLOITING YOUR OPPONENTS WEAKNESS

Allen Fox advises, "Your specific plan will normally involve applying constant pressure to an opponent's weakness, either by attacking it or by out steadying it. You hope, thereby, to break the weak stroke down. And if this happens, his strong strokes will probably falter as well. Every part of your game does not have to be better than your opponents for you to break him down. All you have to do is find an exchange where you have a relative advantage and work on it over and over until your opponent cracks. There is an analogy in warfare. Alexander the Great's favourite tactic was a ferocious frontal assault. He used this with tremendous success, even against armies that outnumbered his by more than ten to one. His plan was to apply overwhelming force to a particular point in his enemy's line, destroy that section of the line , and create a panic which would spread throughout the enemy army."

Fox also points out that if the opponent is playing his shots to your weakness but your weakness is still stronger than your opponent's weakest shot then continue trading shots from your weakness to his weakness as you will still come out top.

USEFUL TIPS

This book is about the psychology of tennis rather than about how to hit a tennis stroke correctly so I do not want to go into detail in this latter area. I have, therefore, just provided a short list of tips here that will be beneficial to you and assuming you hadn't already realised or learnt about them then these should increase the chance of you winning. Each of the below are massively important and should be used on court whenever you play:-

- Vary where your serve goes.
- Look to wrong-foot your opponent.
- If you are being out rallied – try charging the net.
- Hit deep to the opponent's weakest shot.
- The ultimate cardinal sin is to do a double fault in a tie break. Concentrate on getting your first serve in even if it means slowing it down a little.
- Make your opponent run. Rather than just having one thing to think about, i.e. hitting the ball, this gives him two things to think about i.e. hitting the ball whilst running. It throws out his timing and doesn't allow him to grove a shot.
- If in doubt play your most reliable shot.
- The nearer your opponent stands in to receive your serve, the more effective the body serve is.
- If your opponent doesn't have great movement then a serve at the body can be very effective. Don't forget about this shot.
- If a person is running around his backhand, for example, and you are having difficulty getting it to his backhand then play a shorter shot, with the same direction, as it is harder to run round.
- If you are a hacker (I'm talking about one who hits the ball correctly not that plays moon balls) and are getting your shots in so regularly that you rarely miss a shot then try something obvious out. Try hitting the ball harder and see if it continues to go in. If your technique is correct then you will probably find that the number of points you lose by making mistakes is lower than the number you start to win due to

the increased speed of your shots. You will also feel pretty pleased with yourself that you can hit the ball significantly harder.

- To generate more power in your shots, you can increase your arm speed, snap your wrist more, lengthen your backswing or swivel your body round more when playing the shot.
- If you find that a lot of your shots are going slightly long each time then if feasible, aim more of your shots diagonally rather than straight so that the distance you have to hit into is greater. You will find that the same shots will probably go in. Consider the maths behind it:-

Court length 78 feet
Court width 36 feet
Diagonal length 85.9 feet

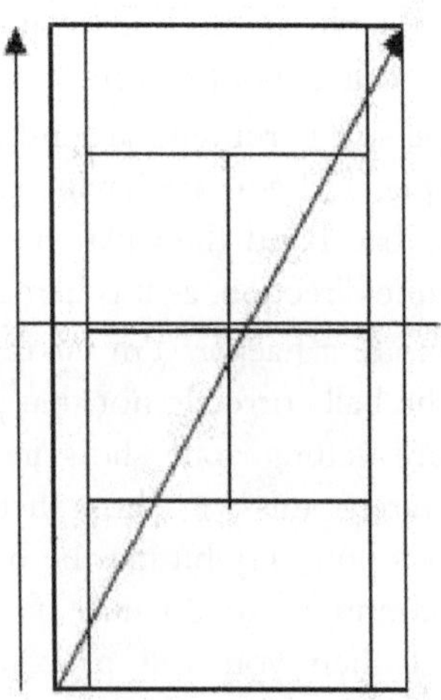

Fig 12 Court dimensions

So the difference between hitting diagonally across court compared to hitting straight down the court is an extra 8 metres, which is over 10% more court length to hit into. Also bear in mind that the net is lower in the centre of the court compared to down the lines, so it gives you a greater margin for error.

- In 'Tennis' by Van Raalte and Silver-Bernstein they advise, "Against power players one of the most effective strategies is to change the pace of the ball. Hit a hard shot, and then follow it with a soft shot. If you can hit slice or topspin, try adding that to the mix. Changing the pace breaks up your opponents rhythm."
- Brad Gilbert in 'Winning Ugly' advises the same approach that Ivan Lendl adopts, saying, "Start below your maximum pace and rhythm in your first few games. Don't try to cream those early shots. Let yourself build into a solid, comfortable 'power' rhythm. It'll happen if you let yourself resist the temptation to hit hard and win quick."
- If you hit a lot of topspin forehands then instead of hitting up the back of the ball (i.e. vertically) try hitting across the ball (horizontally). It will cause the ball to move sideways by a couple of metres and can confuse some opponents. This is called the inside-out forehand.
- We see players who, having missed a shot, rehearse the correct way of playing it. Logic dictates that the more times you practice hitting the ball in the correct way the more likely that it

will become your natural instinct so this technique is be worth adopting.

- If you are playing against a player or players who just get everything back and are camped on the baseline then the best way to beat them is to get to the net to aim for the smash put away. Your aim is to unsettle them by attacking.
- Brad Gilbert advises, "When someone starts attacking you at the net it's human nature to watch them and not the tennis ball. But the player isn't attacking you, the ball is. The player doesn't come over the net, the ball does. Watch the ball. Concentrate totally on the ball. Good contact is almost impossible when you're watching the attacking player with one eye and the ball with the other." So when you are playing your shot there needs to be a shift change so that at the correct point in time you switch off the peripheral vision that watches the movement of your opponent and your entire focus is on the ball".
- On a windy day use the wind to your advantage. You need to accept that the ball could move considerably right up to the instant that you have to hit your shot and therefore your total concentration is key. You need to be on your toes and able to adjust your feet in an instant. Van Raalte and Silver-Bernstein comment, "On windy days especially, the mentally alert player is the one who has the edge." Allen Fox also highlights the lob as a key weapon in the wind, "The wind becomes an enormous factor on the lob. Lob offensively against the wind. Using the wind properly can turn your lob into a diabolical

weapon. When your opponent comes to the net with the wind at his back, the first shot to think of, if you are not too rushed by his approach, is an offensive lob. You can hit the ball rather hard so that it goes quickly over his head, and the wind will slow the ball so it drops into the court. A strong wind will give you tremendous leeway on this shot. You can swing with some abandon and hardly miss. If the volleyer closes in to his normal position, he will be helpless against this shot". So next time it's windy think about the positives, don't complain about the conditions.

- If you are at the net and have got yourself out of position midpoint then it is not unusual for indecision and a bit of panic to set in. In such situations you don't always feel there is time to look around to see which side your partner is on (so you can cover the other side). In such situations you are often better choosing one side or the other straight away and getting there quickly. The reason for this is that as your partner is stood behind you he can quite clearly see which side you are covering so he can cover the other side. Your partner has more time than you to move due to him being further back as well. The one thing you need to make sure you don't do is dither particularly down the centre of the court. It is sensible to make this point before you play with a new partner so if he suddenly sees you dart to one side or the other when you are at the net then he can see if he needs to switch sides.

- Anticipation is key in doubles. Former tennis great Jack Kramer stated, "In commenting on the qualifications for the ideal doubles player, I would like to emphasize a factor which is all too often overlooked. The thing which separates the great from the near-great doubles players is the uncanny ability to anticipate the actions of their opponents. This art is not well understood by the average doubles player, especially the youngsters."
- You win the toss and elect to serve first. Your partner lets you serve. Three minutes later you have lost your service game. Sound familiar? It probably does. Most club players don't possess a reliable 120mph serve which wins them a game single-handedly. Don't be surprised if you lose that first service game of the match. Your opponents are at a very high concentration level as the match starts and they have nothing to lose. You are under pressure as you don't want to lose face by losing your first service game. Why don't you keep a record of your success rate when you serve first against a record of when you let your opponent serve first and compare the stats. If you find that you are having more success in letting your opponent serve first then the logical step is to serve second. In Brad Gilberts book 'Winning Ugly' he explains why he believes it is sensible to serve after your opponent, not before:-
    1. It gives you additional time to loosen up, to relax into the match.
    2. Your opponent will take it as an insult because by letting him serve you are

saying you don't fear or rate his serve. This will cause your opponent to hit harder which reduces the consistency and also the effectiveness of the serve.

3. One of the easiest times to break serve is on your opponent's first service of the match. As discussed earlier if it is harder for you to win your first service game in the first game of the match then the same logic applies to your opponent.
4. If your opponent holds serve then you haven't lost a thing – the match is still on serve.

The only downside of Gilberts theory of letting your opponent serve first is that he may believe it to be a sign that your service is weak however as your service will not differ from normal this probably won't make too much difference.

Gilbert summarises by saying, "Instead of starting the match with the idea that you'll work your way into it, begin with the goal of working your opponent out of it".

6 RUNNING A TEAM - MANAGEMENT

DON'T GIVE EVERYONE A GAME

There are essentially two ways to run a team. The first is to aim to win every match possible and do as well as you can. The second is to give everyone a game and to play for fun. My advice to you is that if you are a person who believes in the latter method then you need to consider changing your method. There are a number of reasons for this:-

- People enjoy winning rather than losing. If you play to win then it is likely the team you put out will be as good a team as you can get out which gives you more chance of winning and therefore the happier your players will be and they will therefore be keener to play again.

- Having aims and goals will produce better results. There is a reason why the whole of society is built upon a hierarchical model with targets (i.e. pretty much all of us have a boss who sets objectives) because it is proven to work and running a tennis team is no different. Tell your players what your overall goal is for the match. You may even break this down into what you would like the individual team members or pairs to achieve – this is a judgement call though
- Humans by their nature like to bond and on a tennis court if they feel they are one half of a partnership then it makes the experience that much more enjoyable. By contrast if players continually have different tennis partners because you are constantly rotating the team all the time then it is very difficult to get any kind of bond, rhythm or partnership going.
- If a team is difficult to get into then when a player who does not normally get into the side gets a game then not only does it give him a high but will make him try his hardest to play as well as he possibly can in order to try and get in the side the following week.
- People have very busy lives with family commitments so they want to make sure the time and effort they are putting in on court is going towards a goal.
- If players are playing regularly for the team then they are likely to commit more to the team and place the teams matches higher on their importance scale then if it is just a match every few weeks.

- Giving everyone a go in the team means that players don't have to fight for their places so they don't have to perform to the best of their ability.
- Most players need to play at least twice a week in order to play to maintain their level. If they are swapped in and out of the team then their standard of play will drop.
- If you decide to give everyone a game but try to compromise by playing the better players against the better opposition teams and the weaker against the weaker teams then you could have a situation where you win the tougher matches but lose the weaker matches. The better players could refuse to play when they realise what is happening as they are used to playing to win and will be able to see that their inclusion in matches will be a waste of time because matches are being thrown elsewhere.

HOW TO WIN EVERY MATCH YOU PLAY

Regardless of the size of club you play at and therefore the resources available to you from a player perspective you always need to work at making sure your team is the best it can be. This chapter is essentially aimed at captains of teams at small or medium sized clubs as these are in the majority. The advice here is of slightly less relevance to captains of teams where they already have a huge pool of the best players in the region at their disposal, however even if that is the case there may be areas of interest.

Let's assume it's possible to calculate in percentage

terms the improvement a player can make in his game. Let's assume one of your regular team players has some coaching over a number of months and this improves his game by 10% and during the same period he works on his fitness in the gym giving him another 5 % and finally he gets psychological match training giving him another 5%, then this is a small increase to your team's strength. However, if you manage to persuade someone who currently doesn't play for your team such as a top player from another club who is 100% better than the player who has had all the training then we are talking much larger gains. There may even be players within your own club who have opted not to play for certain teams but may with some persuasion play one match and then go on from there. Often the club coach has got into the habit of just doing nothing but coaching however he might be talked into turning out for your team. The biggest source of quality players however will always be from other clubs.

The purists may argue against the philosophy of 'bringing in' players rather than trying to improve existing players however your aim as captain should always be to put out the best team you can each time you play. Just as a very weak player in a four person team will almost guarantee you can't win a match but can only draw at best, then a very good player can guarantee you a win or a draw in every match.

It is all about getting good players through the door and if you want to do well then this is what you need to concentrate on. This is the same in all sports and at all levels. Consider the philosophy of football manager Sir

Alex Ferguson. The only players he will buy are those who he believes are currently the best in the world or are young and will in his opinion become the best in the world. Good players attract good players. You will also find, when running a tennis team that once you start getting two or three committed strong players through the door then it makes the job easier to attract more good players.

Each club will normally have a number of captains within the club with each running a team. To ensure your club continue to recruit high quality players in a conveyor belt fashion then a mindset needs to be established not just in each captain's head but also in their player's. The mindset is for the captains and their players to always be on the lookout for new players wherever they are because better players can be anywhere. One example I can give is when our men's captain told me he had been chatting to a girl at a party who played tennis. He used his charms to get her down to the club and have a mixed four with us. She lived quite a distance away but she could see that we had a young, sociable team and she was happy to travel a bit further to play for our mixed team. She was a great addition.

As explained though, the easiest place to find quality players is at other clubs so the task is to persuade them to join yours. This may not always be a popular thing to do however a player will only move if they want to. Much better that this player joins your team rather than someone elses. The best approach is to chat away with a target player generally making him familiar with you and your teammates. You may even invite him for a hit by saying you need a player to stand in this week in your regular four. It is all about getting him used to your club, you and your teammates until he is comfortable. Make sure that if you are unlikely to see him again for a while that you get some way of contacting him there and then.

Another excellent way is to invite an opposition player to play in a tournament with you. I have used this numerous times to try and get good players familiar with me, used to representing our club and then eventually to join our team. A typical path I have used before which has achieved the result of getting a new player on board is:

1. Impress him with your play and your team's play.
2. Be friendly and chat with him.
3. Ask him if he would be interested in making up a four if you are short of a player.
4. Get contact details.
5. Contact him a week later to get him to play in your 'regular four' telling him that a player has dropped out. The 'four' could of course be arranged specifically for him.
6. At the next tournament invite him to play with you – he would be representing your club.
7. Start dropping into conversation the idea of him playing at your club and playing for your team.

Sometimes a pursuit can take some time but getting that key player can be worth the wait.

In summary therefore, if you want to win every match, then ensure the strongest players in the league join your team and get them playing in as many of the matches as they can.

LOSING ONE PLAYER A YEAR

Players come and go at clubs. The majority of reasons why players will no longer be able to play for the team will be outside your control as captain such as players moving out of the area, family commitments etc. The only times when you, as captain, will have an influence is if you are either a very bad captain and repel the players or a very good one and therefore attract them. Whatever the reason for players leaving, you need to budget to lose one player per year for every six team players available. If you don't factor this in then the team will get weaker and weaker over the years. If you have set this expectation then you know that you will need to get one new player every year by whatever means you can.

So how do you go about recruiting new players? One way is to go to your current players and ask them if they know anyone who might consider joining. It is likely that each player will have a network of players they have played with in the past or play with presently so you are immediately tapping into a fair size market.

Other ideas for recruiting players are asking if people can put up notices at their work asking for interested players.

Don't underestimate the power of attraction either. Good looking men attract women and good looking women attract men.

Another route that can be taken is the idea of feeder clubs or a club sharing arrangement. These are usually only useful if clubs have teams in different region's leagues but as tennis captain how about putting a proposal to your club committee that team players from another club can play for your team to help you out if you are struggling and vice versa. The request to the committee would be that the players don't pay an annual payment, just the match fee, but the club classifies them as members, if this is the only way they can play under league rules. One carrot to dangle to the committee is that it increases the opportunity for getting this high quality player to join the club in future years if the player enjoys it. Naturally the issue has to be handled carefully as membership and money are involved here. Sometimes a treasurer or club secretary who is onside can be useful in these situations.

THE PURSUIT

The ideal for a captain is to attract players who are not just very good tennis players but who are young and have a personality which will fit with the existing team members. Getting the right person therefore is not easy and requires patience. From my own experience there have been a couple of players who I have carefully and subtly tapped up over the course of two years before eventually persuading them to join the club and team. Very often a player will rebuff advances of joining another club for a variety of reasons however the one thing true to almost every tennis player in the world is that if you and your club are well respected then that player will be flattered. Care has to be taken not to nag the player over and over; it's all about getting the right balance. As you may only see your target player twice a season in the home and away matches against that person's club you need to talk to him each time. As some of your players will get the chance to speak to the target player, for example when sat off waiting for the other pairs to finish their match, then get them to speak to him about joining the club as well. The level of flattery that the player feels will be even higher now as he begins to feel popular and that he is effectively being head hunted. He will also be of the view that he will be able to easily fit into the team as he knows that the players in the team want him to join.

When chatting to the target player about joining your club, part of your conversation needs to focus on the player's current situation within his club in order to establish when the best time is to start pushing him a little more. This can be the long part where patience is required. Although a player might be happy with his club at present, things will very often take a turn for the worse over time for example if a new captain comes in and starts causing issues. All you can do in the monitoring phase is to chat with him casually about how things are going at his club, how he is feeling about his club and what his relationship with his team captain is, for example finding out if his captain values him highly and picks him in each match.

If you eventually strike lucky and find that he is unhappy, then the best technique you can employ is to ask him about what is going badly with his club and encourage him to speak about why he feels unsettled over it. At this point say again to him, "well, the offer is still there to join us if you want". If he is unhappy you may well get the response you have been after.

THE WORMHOLE

Never underestimate the pulling power of one individual. Ten years ago four members of our club had a weekly indoor mixed game and one particular week one of the players was unable to get there in time so it left only three of them. Fortunately they managed to persuade a player who had been leaving a different court to make up the four. The player who stayed and made up the four played for a different club in a different region, one which unusually had no mixed league. They had very strong ladies' and men's teams and a lot of these players wanted to play mixed but couldn't. The player who made up the four got on very well with our players and they swapped contact numbers. Players from this new player's club then started coming over and playing mixed for our team as they didn't have a team of their own. A virtual wormhole was effectively then established between the clubs which were located fifty miles apart. In time the original lady who had stood in for that four moved away from the area however her legacy remained because the relationship between the two clubs continued. Some players who now travel over had never met the original lady but still play for us as the wormhole has been kept open.

TRANSFORMATION OF THE FOOTBALLER TO THE TENNIS PLAYER

There have been many occasions where people join a tennis club having never picked up a racket or who have played at school a few years before and wish to give it a go again. Many of these players are in their twenties and play other sports. I have seen these players start playing in tennis matches for other clubs and they are often embarrassed due to their lack of experience and technique even after having played a handful of matches. Over the course of the next couple of years however you can clearly see the enormous improvement in their play. The style of their play is usually poor (as most do not get coaching) but after the first year of matches they have got rid of their insecurities on court and have found that due to their superior fitness, their physical strength and their speed (due to their age) they are getting results.

Players will often turn up to play at a club time for the first time wearing football tops and black trainers and existing club members often look down their nose at them and try to usher them out of the club as soon as they can. This is a huge mistake however as here you have the chance to move someone from another sport into tennis and most importantly you can bring more youth into the club. Young players particularly in their twenties, for example, have all the raw materials that have been mentioned earlier i.e. fitness, strength and speed. They will chase every ball down and before long the only people to whom they are losing consistently are the ones who are technically superior tennis players. Within a reasonable period of time they will be beating the players who originally looked down their nose at them.

Don't underestimate how keen people can become when they get involved in a club. This may begin with them just coming down to club time to begin with but as their standard improves they will become more and more keen and then naturally progress into playing in matches. Some players, who some at your club feel shouldn't be allowed to join based on their initial impression, may actually be the future captains of your teams and could stick around for the next ten years.

From a financial perspective for your club, assuming your clubs annual membership fee is £100 then if a member joins for 10 years which is quite probable, then it is £1000 towards club funds. Another great reason to get as many people playing at your club as possible.

In most tennis clubs all the focus is on junior's or the regular senior's weekly club sessions, not many clubs focus on bringing the twenty year olds back into the game but here is a very useful niche market and where one person comes in he can also bring his friends too. So if a player in his twenties comes to your club time and can barely hit the ball over the net and is dressed ready to play rugby – welcome him with open arms and help him to be the best player he can be. If he needs coaching then take him to the side and politely suggest it. As long as you are polite and reassure him then he will hopefully take your advice, get coaching whilst continuing coming to your club sessions and improving.

BRINGING IN A RINGER

If you are running a team then there will often be times, particularly if you are at a small club, when you are short of a player and have a choice of resorting to a very weak player at your club or bringing a ringer in, in other words a strong player from outside your club. If you decide to go down the morally correct route by selecting a very weak player from your club then you will no doubt damage his confidence, annoy his partner, annoy the rest of the team due to losing the match, weaken your league position and feel like you have wasted your time organising the match in the first place as the result was a foregone conclusion. Even the opposition may not enjoy it as much because they won't get a decent game although they probably won't mind if they get an easy win.

The alternative to this is to bring in a ringer; definitely the best option!

To do this it helps to have as broad a knowledge as possible of the other teams in not just your league but other leagues in your area as well. The best way to get this knowledge is to switch clubs occasionally (this can keep you fresh and you meet a lot of new people too) or join more than one club. Switching clubs shouldn't be done too often but is a great way of gaining knowledge of other players. If you are going to change clubs then you might as well switch to a club that has teams in a different league. If you end up being captain of a team at your current club then having had experience at another local club and the contacts you have built up in that club can be of massive benefit.

So assuming you are now captain, begin by persuading a good player from a different league to play for you (make sure he doesn't play for another team in your league as he will be ineligible) preferably who the opposition who you are about to play are unlikely to know. Speak to the borrowed player before the match and tell him to ensure he doesn't let the opposition know that he is not a member of your club. Ensure also that your team are fully briefed that you are bringing in a ringer so none of your team put you in an awkward situation. You may also need to advise any of your spectators and obviously need to get to them as soon as they walk through the gate. You need of course to be conscious of the moral opinions of your team members as well as they may not agree with this practice. In this situation just tell them the ringer has just joined the club. It keeps everyone happy!

Bringing a ringer in should only really be done as a last resort and I would never advocate doing it when you have good players within your club who are quite capable of holding their own in matches. If the only other options are calling off the match or wasting everyone's time with a player who can barely hit the ball over the net then it can't be too bad a thing. Just make sure no one finds out!

I have to admit to even mooting the idea of borrowing a player from another club within the same league and changing the players name on the form so the league secretary doesn't spot it but have always felt this would be cheating due to the changing of the name. Also there would always be too much of a chance of being caught. For this reason I have never gone ahead with it and I wouldn't recommend it!

In the same way that you may consider bending the rules it is worth keeping an eye out as to whether the opposition are breaking the rules. If there are new players in an opposition team then do some digging. Are they actually members of the club they are playing for and if not are they therefore breaking the leagues rules? Do they play for any other club which has a team in the league and therefore might have played for two teams in the same season breaching league rules? Are they entering a different name on the scorecard? Although the latter example is unlikely, there is no doubt this will have happened many times up and down the country in the past.

SEARCHING FOR THE NEXT TEAM CAPTAIN

This section doesn't refer to searching for someone to succeed you if you are currently captain, it relates to a continual search for as many people who are keen to take on the responsibility and workload of captaincy regardless of which team it is e.g. junior, women's or veterans' captain. Your club will always benefit more if someone (such as yourself) can take a more ambassadorial role within the club (we discuss this in the next section) and look at where a particular person could fit into a club regardless of whether someone is in the position already. You can keep the potential captain waiting in the wings without him knowing your intentions as there is one thing for sure in club tennis the turnover rate for captains is high so scouting for future captains regardless of the position in the club is sensible planning.

One thing that shouldn't be underestimated is how important a team captain is. A good team captain can attract players to the club. If he attracts ten players to the club, then on the basis of £100 annual membership per person, this brings in £10,000 over ten years; a very tidy sum with most of it being clear profit. Added to this a good captain is usually enthusiastic and will often attend and perhaps organise social events. As team players are always the strongest players at a club then the standard of club time tennis will be improved as well by having the team players playing. Often at clubs there can be complaints of team players not joining in and participating enough. It should be viewed in the opposite way by regular club members namely that when team players do turn up it is a bonus for the regulars as they get to play against better players.

The enthusiastic team captain is worth his weight in gold and can come from almost anywhere. Encourage regular team players to have a go at being the captain and see how they do.

CLUB CAPTAIN

Some clubs have a Club Captain who not only captains one team but effectively oversees all the teams. Having someone in this position can be of great benefit for the performance of the teams. Taking on this job presents challenges in itself as no one (such as the other team captains) likes to have their toes trodden on however if the person is right then that person can guide the club and teams in the right direction without causing any problems.

The Club Captain often oversees a number of areas. If a club and its teams are very success orientated and the aim is to win as many titles as possible in a season, then a decision needs to be made on which leagues the teams play in, for example, if one league is weaker than another does the club put a particular team in the weak one in order to win silverware or in the tougher league where they probably won't but where the players will improve as they are playing against better players week in, week out. Alternatively does the club enter a team in each? Although the club or committee may make the final decision on which leagues a team might enter the Club Captain has a very important role to play. A good Club Captain will know the strengths of the respective leagues at anytime and so can steer the decision.

Often a strategic decision might be made regarding where the club wants to concentrate its efforts. An example might be that a club has two ladies' teams where on occasion the same ladies are needed for both teams. Often during the season there will be fixture clashes and both team captains want the same player. Let's assume we have League A which has five divisions and League B which has four divisions. In League A you have a ladies team in division two and the club has made a decision at the start of the season that the priority is to try and win promotion to division one. In League B the other ladies team is in division three and would struggle to get promoted but should be able to stay up without too much effort. The Club Captain is often needed to ensure during the course of the season that this aim is not forgotten, in the same way that a project manager in business has the task of ensuring the project stays on course. Team captains are naturally going to fight to get the players they want playing for their team however if by not sticking to the original plan both sides end up staying in the same division instead of one getting promoted, then it's been a wasted season. The role of the Club Captain here is crucial as he is the one that has to remind the team captain of the ladies' team that is playing in League B that priority goes to the team in League A and that in the event of a clash of fixtures the League A team needs the key players. A large amount of diplomacy is needed in this instance but again it is where a good Club Captain comes in very handy.

As mentioned, at larger clubs there may be a specific person whose job it is to carry this out, for example the head coach, however at smaller clubs this is often not the case but that is not to say that someone should not take on the job in an unofficial capacity and put forward his ideas at the Annual General Meeting. In the example we have used you may have the choice of playing in a weaker league and winning silverware or playing in a stronger league and improving your tennis, or a mix of both. Someone needs to be thinking about what is best overall.

CAN I BEND THIS NEW RULE?

Regardless of the league or sport you are in, the person(s) who control the league will always introduce new rules or change existing rules. Instead of thinking of this as just another piece of bureaucracy think about whether you can gain any competitive advantage from this change or new rule. Two students of this type of thinking in the football world are Sam Allardyce off the pitch and Thierry Henry on the pitch.

An example of Allardyce's thinking related to when the offside rule was changed so that a player could stand in an offside position without being flagged as offside just as long as he wasn't interfering with play. Allardyce used this to his advantage by getting a player to stand in an offside position to unsettle the opposition defence. All of a sudden the opposition defenders had something new to contend with that they hadn't thought of, they had a player standing behind them and therefore had a choice of leaving him standing there unmarked or the whole defence retreating deeper and therefore putting them on the back foot.

Thierry Henry was a great exponent of finding ways of giving himself an advantage. At free kicks he would ask the referee whether he could take the free kick straightaway or whether he had to wait for the referee's whistle. If the referee told him that the free kick could be taken without him blowing the whistle then before the opposition had had chance to organise their wall and with the keeper out of position Henry would curl the ball into the open net and the referee would have to stand by his decision regardless of the protests by the opposition that they weren't ready.

Both these are examples of staying within the rules but giving yourself an advantage over the opposition. If you are a captain of the tennis team, have you read the league rules? Whether you are captaining a team for the first time or whether you have been doing it for a number of years, one of the first things you must do before the season starts is read through the rules not just to check you are adhering to the regulations but also to see if you can gain an advantage. If you are unsure about something or wish to check that an advantage would stand up under the league rules, speak to the official in charge and get his confirmation on an email and then take advantage of this rule.

Allardyce looks for loopholes that the authorities may not have thought of, he will then spend time practising with his team how an advantage can be gained. Due to the public nature of professional sport any item of interest is broadcast immediately for all to see. If a loophole is exploited to a side's advantage then within a game or two, every other club either tries the same thing and/or starts working at dealing with it happening against them, thus minimising the advantage. As most of us do not play tennis in front of cameras then the only way of communication is by word of mouth between opposition teams, a much slower route, meaning you can use any advantage you have many times before others catch on.

Remember any advantage you can exploit may only make a small difference perhaps 1% or 2% but the one thing we all know in tennis is that close matches can be won or lost by the smallest of details, for example a ball landing two centimetres to the left or right can, decide a result. No possible advantage therefore should be ignored. Have a read through the rules and see if you can spot any opportunities.

WHO PLAYS ON WHICH SIDE?

A partnership playing together for the first time has a few basic decisions to decide before the spin for service is made. These include deciding whether they should serve if they win the toss, which one of them should serve first and who should receive on which side (deuce or advantage).

As with anything in life there is rarely one answer that suits all, however it is about playing the odds and unless an exceptionally good argument can be put forward to the contrary, the strongest server of the two should always serve first and the strongest player should always receive in the advantage court.

There might be an occasional exception to the rule with regard to who receives in the advantage court. An example would be if one player in a pair is left handed and one is right handed (so both players would be playing on the forehand side or both on the back hand side). It is often the case that both would prefer to play on their forehand side, however if the weaker player is the left handed one then this would mean that person would be receiving on the advantage side, thus going against the recommendation. However if the alternative is switching round so that both receive on their backhand side, and that is deemed to be an even weaker position, then it may well be better to put both players on their forehand side (with the weaker player receiving in the advantage court). This way both players will be playing the majority of the match on their forehand side which is usually their stronger.

Many players like to play on a particular side; a right-handed player would often prefer to play on the deuce court, due to his forehand being stronger. Which side the players play on is extremely important though, particularly when you are to play in a match.

In tennis a partnership will usually be made up of one player being stronger than the other. There is also often the scenario where one player of the four on court is significantly stronger than the other three players. A significantly stronger player, who might find it all a bit easy, can often because of this, be prone to lapses in concentration. As this scenario, of a players concentration levels varying, can be quite common then it is worth us considering the effect of concentration levels on the scoreline.

We examine the subconscious thoughts going through the stronger players head in two scenarios, firstly with him receiving in the deuce court and secondly receiving in the advantage court.

STRONGER PLAYER PLAYING IN THE DEUCE COURT

Action

Score is deuce and opponent serves to stronger player [Subconscious thought of the stronger player: I don't need to put full concentration in here as it's not game point (let's say the player's concentration level is at 60%)]

Result

Due to the strong player not trying his hardest the pair lose the point

Action

Opposition then serve to weaker player who is in the advantage court and due to him being weak he is unable to return the serve

Result
Game lost

STRONGER PLAYER RECEIVING IN THE ADVANTAGE COURT

Action
Score is deuce and opponent serves to weaker player who this time is in the deuce court

Result
Due to him being weak he is unable to return the serve

Action
Opposition then serve to stronger player in the advantage court. As it is game point his concentration is at 100%. He is the strongest player on the court and wins the point

Result
Deuce

This is one of the most common scenarios in tennis. It is the difference in mind-set that players have when they are faced with game point rather than a non-game point. At game point a stronger player will often thrive under this relatively small amount of pressure as he has a challenge. If he is game point down he sees himself as the person who can rescue the situation and who everyone can depend on or if it is game point to him and his partner he has a chance for glory. Therefore, by recommending the stronger player plays on the advantage side you are maximising his concentration level and giving him the best chance of staying in or winning the game. In the example above assuming the weaker player is concentrating at 100% in both scenarios (as the self-conscious weaker player often does) then we are talking a 20% difference in concentration between the two players over the two points. The percentages used here are obviously not measurable in real terms but are purely used as an example to assist the reader with understanding the benefits of maximising the strengths in the partnership.

Hopefully this example has shown that the key to success is to get your concentration level for every point in the game to the level it would be if it were game point. This can often be very hard to do when the score is 15-0 or 15-15 but if you are able to think in this way and train your mind to concentrate at this level then you will have an advantage over your opponent who will often be careless at the beginning of a game.

There is nothing more demoralising to a server who has won a large number of deuce points in a row but can't finish the game because he is up against a strong player who keeps hitting winning returns on the advantage side. Even if he ends up winning the service game the player who is serving is always going to be a lot more tired than the receivers. By deciding to put the stronger player on the advantage side therefore the opposition server can be out there serving for quite a long time.

WHO PLAYS 1ST PAIR, 2ND PAIR, 3RD PAIR?

This is not always clear cut as some match formats involve players swapping partners in different sets however assuming we are talking about a three pair team where the partnerships stay the same the standard rule is that the best players play as the first pair, the second best pair as the seconds and the third best as the thirds. However there can be occasions where there is little difference in standard between two or all three of your pairs. In this scenario it is important that the first pair are those players who thrive under tennis pressure, who want to be first pair and who love an audience. These are the usual traits you should look for in your first pair. The third pair are those who do not want to be put under any pressure and who don't want an audience. By arranging the players in their correct partnerships you will maximise their performance.

WHO GETS TO PARTNER THE BEST PLAYER?

Well usually the answer to this one is 'you' after all you are the one who picks who plays with who so surely it's your right and privilege to partner the best player isn't it? Nope, wrong. The problem that arises here is if you aren't very good and are running the team because really it's the only way you are going to get into it. If you are able to recognise that you are weak then you should be able to understand that when the best player in the team says he doesn't mind playing with you, that he is being polite and is in fact lying. The bottom line is that everyone wants the best partner possible and the better players are no different. Very often he will be noble about it and will tell you what you want to hear so you need to be aware of this because by putting a good player with a bad player (assuming you are the weakest player) could end up resulting in the good player dropping out of the team altogether. In short, therefore, the golden rule is to put your best players together unless there is some obvious reason why this is not a good idea for example if they don't get on.

On the other hand if you are running the team and are a weak player but are unable to recognise this fact then you are the type of player who is disliked at every club up and down the country!

Experts will always recommend not splitting your strengths and that putting your best players together will always provide the best results for the team. In certain circumstances this might not always be the case but more often than not it is and if you are in doubt then always put your best players together. They are fully aware that they should win all their matches, therefore you are providing them with the challenge they need.

USEFUL TIPS

- Players can range in temperament. You can have a fiery character where he tends to attack and then at the other end of the spectrum a very mellow player whose game might centre around defensive play. When picking teams there can therefore be a number of combinations. If you don't have all attacking players then often a successful one will be the fire and water combination, i.e. one attacking and one defensive. One that you should avoid, particularly in men's doubles is the water and water combination. Two steady but defensive players will always struggle.

- Tell your team that the match starts ten minutes before it does so that they are on time and you don't get stressed due to players turning up late.
- One technique that Hamburg Football Club used in their successful European football reign in the seventies was to play a five-a-side match immediately prior to the actual match so the players were match tight from the very start and if a chance came to one of their players in the first minute he wouldn't miss it due to not being ready. Naturally this requires superior fitness but fitness can be easily worked on. Applying this theory to your tennis team why not get the members of your team playing a doubles (and a singles as well if it is a six person team) game where you are actually keeping score. You only need to play a couple of games and your players will have essential match focus which will then be there from the start in a match.
- Each player has a preference as to which side (i.e. the deuce or the advantage court) that he prefers to play on but try to encourage your players to play an even number of times on each side during the course of the season. This will then help iron out any weaknesses and also stop

any new weaknesses developing due to a player covering up his weakest shots. If players play in two teams during the course of the season then it might be sensible for them to try playing in the advantage court for one team and the deuce court in the other so it makes them get an even balance. It does of course depend on their partners requirements too.

Although being captain can be very rewarding it can also be a very stressful and soul destroying job at times. If you do enjoy the highs but also suffer the hassles then make sure you give yourself a break each year. Instead of running both the summer and winter teams then just run one of them and give yourself that time to rest and to feel that you actually miss running the summer team so that you are raring to go when summer comes around again. This also applies with tennis in general. Ensure you have a period each year where you don't play. It will give your body as well as your mind time to recover and will renew your enthusiasm.

7 RUNNING A TEAM – MOTIVATIONAL/PSYCHOLOGICAL TIPS

PRE-SEASON GET-TOGETHER

Firstly, prior to beginning a tennis season, it is good to take stock of where you are as a squad. If you have a large squad and will be rotating it throughout the season then having a regular practice night is a good idea in order to get your players playing regularly. If you have a small squad then a minimum of one pre-season get-together is a must. It is not necessarily key to have more than one because unless you are rotating your squad throughout the season your players will start to get fed up with playing tennis at about the three quarter stage of the season. If you insist on them playing too many pre-season games they will have had enough even as early as mid-way through the season. It is however a fine balancing act between too many practises and making sure the players are ready for the first match. If you feel the first match will be fairly routine then this can be used almost as a warm up, however if you are facing a tough first match then perhaps more than one pre-season hit is sensible.

If you are fortunate enough or have worked hard enough to have a good size squad then you may be in the ideal position of sending out an invite to all your squad advising them of the time and date when there is a squad practice and not have to chase them up, safe in the knowledge that enough will turn up to be able to have a good team session. If on the other hand you do have the squad but they are poor at responding to invites then it is worth putting the effort in to contact them individually to see if they are able to come along. The pre-season get-together is massively important. If you get a large number of people of a good standard attending it makes future events easier to arrange because the players know that you deliver on your promises, they know they will get a good game and if you organise it in a fun way they should enjoy themselves. It shows that the club is thriving, the squad is strong and that there is competition for places which makes everyone try harder. The third scenario is when the squad is small and it is just a case of having to contact each player directly and organising a four for example. This in itself is just as good and can be the first step towards building a squad.

Once you have everyone together then making it light hearted but with some competition is the key. No doubt in your group you will have a coach or two who will have a number of good ideas for games to play from past experience to use in this situation. If no one comes up with any ideas then how about appointing two players (who have a lot of banter with each other) as team captains (especially ones who aren't the best players as this will boost their confidence) and bill it on your invite as 'The Big Match: Chris Select IV v Jenny Select IV'. Another alternative is having an American tournament where players get to play with different partners. The day should always involve players partnering different players because as the league matches occur thick and fast, and players are not always available, you may have to put players together who have never partnered each other. At least if they have had a few games together in a pre-season hit then it removes the excuse of, "we've never played together before". Even if they don't get to play together in the practice but at least meet and chat, it means they have something they can refer back to which helps them to feel more comfortable on court.

To close out the pre-season get-together any good captain will try and get the players to go to the pub. Some people will be keen to go whereas others will dither a little. As team captain the ditherers are looking to you to be told what they should be doing so make a point of saying confidently to everyone that the plan is to nip to the pub for a quick drink afterwards. If you can get people chatting and bonding they end up enjoying the day that much more.

LISTENING TO YOUR PLAYERS

The only way to get the best out of a player is to know what motivates him to play well and on the flip side what prevents him from playing well. The best person to tell you this information is the player himself. This might come voluntarily but as you need to know this information then it is best to ask him it. Once you are aware of both these pieces of information then as captain or as the player's partner it is your job to ensure that the things that motivate the player are in place and the things that would stop him from playing his best are removed.

PRIMARY LEVEL OF MOTIVATION

My study over the years of players' attitudes going into matches has revealed that their motivation works at two levels. The primary level is the player's core motivation which will not change that much from match to match, for example the captain will usually be highly motivated by the fact it his team and the team's performance reflects on his ability to manage. Another player will play to stay fit and get a bit of competition and again his motivation is the same each match as this aim does not change ie it is his primary level of motivation.

During a tennis club social night, I started a conversation asking our players what each of their three core motivations are for a match and was quite surprised by their responses as some of the responses had never even occurred to me and hadn't been ones I had ever used myself. I was also surprised as I expected each person to at least mention similar ones to those highlighted by the players who had answered before them. Instead each had their own unique primary motivations which were clearly defined in their heads. Typical ones included, enjoying the accolade of playing in front of a crowd, another was trying to beat a player each match that he viewed as better than him, another was just to practice particular shots each tine. I would recommend having the conversation with your team as I guarantee you will be surprised what motivates people and knowing this can definitely be used to your advantage.

SECONDARY LEVEL OF MOTIVATION

The secondary level of motivation is the type that varies from match to match. A simple example would be where one week a player is lining up against a club that he used to play for. It is highly likely that he wants to do everything in his power to win in order to show them that he is doing better now at his new club. In the next match though, a week later, he will be playing against a different club so he no longer has that same motivation, instead a different one may have taken its place.

When there is a secondary level of motivation such as this it usually sits on top of the primary level of motivation so the player still wants to keep fit and get some competition for example. Often however the secondary level can completely dwarf the primary level. In our example here the player's desperation to prove to his former team-mates that he is now a better player makes him forget about using tennis for exercise.

Typical examples of the secondary level are shown below. Each player is motivated by different things so for example in a six player mixed match your individual team members might have the following different aims:

1st Man: To beat a particular opponent who he dislikes

1st Lady: It's a crunch match against our rivals so is desperate to win

2nd Man: To impress the girl he likes on the other team

2nd Lady: To prove to the captain that she is worthy of a place each week

3rd Man: To avoid getting into a rage as this affects his game

3rd Lady: To get better results than the 2nd lady

The example above is purely to show how diverse players' thinking can be, so as captain it's not always possible for you to know exactly what thoughts players have in their head. In the above case each player is positively motivated by something so all of the above examples would improve your players' performances.

As the secondary level of motivation for each player is not always easy to predict and often changes, then the captain's concentration should be on the primary level of motivation of each of his players and what each player can do to improve that, for example improving core fitness. It is also possible to give them a new primary level of motivation. A typical example would be to get the players more involved in how the team is doing, show them the league tables, make sure they understand who the good teams are and who the weaker teams are. Make sure they understand the rules, e.g. the number of teams promoted and relegated. If you build this knowledge up over the course of the season you will see the benefit before your eyes. You are slowly each week adding an important core motivation to the players' psyche, namely their involvement in the team's destiny and therefore giving them the motivation for the team to do well. Other motivations might include appointing a player to be your vice-captain as this instantly gives that person more motivation.

Having said all this, it is still possible to positively affect players' motivations on the secondary level; again it is a case of understanding and listening to your players and choosing the right thing to say. As you saw in the cases above, the team already had their own positive secondary level motivations and therefore the captain's job in this example is to do very little.

CRUNCH KNOWLEDGE

When a crunch set in a match is in progress involving two other members of your team, then as captain, you need to know how you can help them. Questions you need to ask yourself are as follows:

1. If I get the rest of the team or supporters standing at the side of the court cheering our pair on will the pair react positively or negatively?

2. If I get word to our pair on court of how many games they need to win or that the entire match rests on this then will the challenge inspire them or will they crumble under the pressure?
3. If I tell them an untruth that this set doesn't matter, does this positively motivate them by removing the pressure or will it back fire on me as they won't believe there is any reason to try?

Early on in my tennis captaincy days I was in a situation where I was watching members of my team playing a crucial set and did not know the answers to these questions. Not only did this make me feel helpless it also made me feel that as captain I hadn't done my research properly. It was too late at this point in time, with the players being in the middle of the match, for me to find out for example whether they wanted everyone watching them or not.

To counter this situation occurring then the best course of action is to ask each of your players individually, or as a group, the answers to these three questions before the season starts. It is probably best to just casually move the conversation onto this subject rather than being too direct but once you have this information about each player then when a particular pair are playing together and you know that one of the players is inspired by their teammates cheering them on and the other isn't affected either positively or negatively then you would know to round up your team and get them courtside supporting.

Matt Jarvis in 'Sport Psychology' explains that, "the

presence of others (e.g. a crowd) will lead to better performance for expert athletes but a worse performance for novices"

In summary, know your players' minds as well as is possible and bear in mind that they are all motivated by different things. Consider whether, by telling a player that the next set or match is crucial, it will make them crumble or will get them pumped up for it.

POSITIVITY

To get people to listen to you at any time in life, whether in a team sport or not, you need to ensure that what you are saying is worth listening to. People will always choose to listen to people who they can learn from and avoid those people who talk for the sake of talking and add nothing of value. Everyone in life can make good points but few can talk endlessly making one good point after another. Even if a person is able to do this his audience cannot possibly take them all in. It is sensible as captain therefore to make a small number of crucial points just before your players are to go on court. A golden rule is to ensure you don't overload them.

So what is the ideal number of points to make to the team? This should be no more than three. Making just three points should mean that the points will stay with them and providing they are good ones should help them in the match. The frame of mind of your team and their attitude going onto court is very important and your three comments can have a significant effect, they are a great opportunity, so don't waste them. Ensure all these comments are positive from your team's point of view; this can include pointing out the oppositions' weaknesses.

A good captain should always create as positive an environment as possible but should also be able to recognise when a particular player or team is already sufficiently self-motivated and therefore does not need further motivation.

Negative statements or scolding players should be avoided. If absolutely necessary then use a sandwich criticism technique. This technique is one of the most constructive ways of making a point and is done by sandwiching constructive criticism or advice between two compliments, such as, "you hit that forehand well, next time step into it to generate more power, your forehand is definitely improving".

Positive psychology spans all sports. In the book 'Psychology for football' Cale/Forzoni advise to 'decrease the 'but' and increase the 'and' for example, "You played well, but if you can get more first serves in you will have more success" will not be welcomed as much as the statement, "You played well, and if you can get more first serves in you will have more success"

Cale/Forzoni state, "You can motivate players better with kind words than with a whip"

THE ENTHUSIASM SPIRAL AND THE MOOD LEADER

Just as 'Preparation, Preparation, Preparation' is the key statement if you are entering a tournament (we cover this in a later chapter) the key statement if you are the captain of a team is 'Enthusiasm, Enthusiasm, Enthusiasm'. If other members of the team see that the forthcoming match means a lot to you, then their subconscious will say 'if that person thinks this is important then I should put in some effort'. If, for example, you are in a cup competition and have a bye in the first round and so by default you are already through to the quarter final then advertise the fact to your players that the team is in an excellent position as they are in the quarter final. They will automatically become more interested as it feels like they are in the later stages of the tournament even if it is effectively just the first round. Often if you show enthusiasm then your players will feel better about the whole situation and an interesting consequence of this is that they start to say more positive comments about the team's chances and show more enthusiasm themselves which then makes you as captain feel better. This is the Enthusiasm Spiral and can generate an upwardly positive mood within your team.

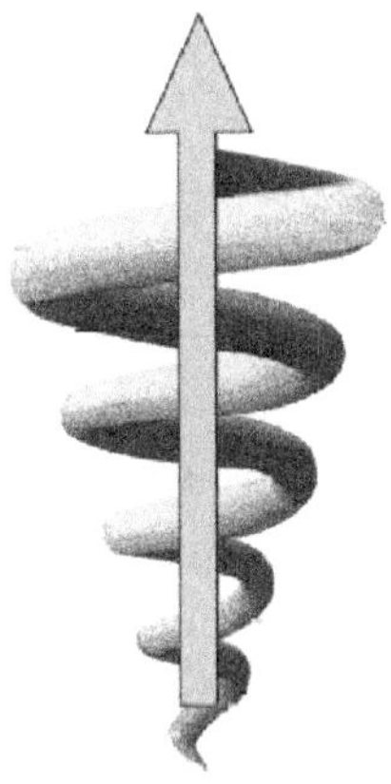

Fig 13 The Enthusiam Spiral

When in amongst a group of people whether tennis related or not, there is often a dominant person. Often that person who can be the star of the show can have varying moods and be more up and down than the others. This person is effectively the Mood Leader so depending on whether they are in a good or bad mood can affect the rest of the group to the point that the whole group have a good or bad time depending on the mood of one person. As team captain whether you feel it's the case or not you are effectively the Mood Leader so if you portray feelings of pessimism, negativity or indifference this will rub off on your team however if you show enthusiasm, positivity and energy then this will increase the chances of this becoming the mood of the team.

Often players will arrive at matches and the first words out of their mouths will be negative comments. As we have covered before you should not be making too many points but instead should target the key areas. Listen to what the player says and what his fears and worries are. Work out what his key issue is and then point him at a positive that negates his worries or moves his focus onto one of his strengths. Sometimes you may need to think about how to turn his fears around so you might ponder it for a few minutes and then work it into a conversation later on or into your pre-match talk.

If a player says he doesn't feel up for that day's match then talk about a match that he recently played well in. Remind him how well he played, what a great win it was, what a fabulous day it was. The more positives the better. Especially with young players you can talk them round and it is very satisfying when you manage to do it. At every opportunity make your players feel competent.

TEAM MOTIVATION

An inherent part of human nature is to be in control. There are three ways of running a team (i) autonomously (ii) letting the team members decide who plays with who (iii) a combination of both. The best way is normally the latter, you should pick the partnerships based on your own judgement looking from the outside as to who you feel play well together but also on occasions take each player to the side and ask them who they like and dislike playing with and then make an informed decision.

A technique that can be used before a crucial match is as follows. If you have an established team with familiar partnerships then suggest to the players that you might mix the players up for a change. Providing you make a suggestion that is not well received by any of the players then the general reaction will be for your players to try to talk you round. At this point you let them do just that and after having a thoughtful moment in front of them agree to keep the pairs as they are normally, as they have suggested. The players, who have suddenly seen a possibility which they didn't particularly like the look of, are now relieved as they are playing with whom they want. They are now far more keen to ensure they succeed because they have been part of the decision process. An inherent part of human nature is to be in control and you have just provided the players with a little bit of control which will benefit the team at the crucial time.

This tactic can often be employed if you have a star player in the team. If you know that the performance of this player has the key bearing on a match then take him to the side and in a similar way give him two possibilities, one that you know he won't go for and one that you know he will. Ask him for his thoughts. More often than not he will be more than happy to give advice and again he will be keen to show you on court that his advice was correct.

There is also a scenario to consider when you have a big match approaching, for example a title clash or a relegation battle. You may have a settled team of players who play in their established partnerships where the players are happy pairing each other, but your strongest players are not playing together. If, however, you have a scenario where you know the team is stronger by the pairs being changed around slightly e.g. when the strongest players are partnering each other, but that these combinations are not that popular with the players, then assuming you have weighed up whether the players can deal with it (without them throwing games through being unhappy) then do the following. Advise all the players of your decision to switch pairs as early as possible so they have time to get used to it and it isn't just thrown upon them that they are partnering a player who isn't their favourite. The best way to prevent this from being an issue is if you mention a few weeks before that this is your plan for the big matches but that for other matches against sides where the result is a foregone conclusion you are happy to keep everyone in their favourite pairs. Players are much happier if they are only stepping out of their comfort zone for a short period. Use this short period wisely therefore at the key times if by doing it the team becomes stronger.

GENERATING A CHALLENGE IF THE OPPOSITION CAN'T

Often in matches you will come across opposition teams and pairs who are vastly weaker than your own team and players. However you may need to not just win the match but also to win by as great a margin as possible to improve your game, set or rubber difference in the league. Your players can easily get bored if not challenged and can end up giving away games cheaply. The key way to motivating them throughout an easy match is to generate some competition seeing as the opposition aren't providing any. If you are in a three pair team then why not wind up one of the other pairs on your team by saying that you will get a better score than them and then after each round ask them how they are doing. Obviously it depends on the characters in your team but if they like a little healthy competition then throw some their way. The fact that they are playing competitive league tennis means that some will want competition so will jump at the chance to have a challenge. If all of your pairs are of a similar standard then see if they agree to the pair getting the lowest scores buying the after-match drinks.

THE LOOK OF DISGUST

Albert Mehrabian cited in 'Sports Coach (2003)' that research suggests over 90% of information is conveyed non-verbally. As captain of your team or as a player's partner beware that you are being watched even when you don't realise it. By something as slight as pulling a negative expression or dropping your shoulders you can demotivate your players or your partner. Bear in mind, spectators can see the faces that you pull and one of these spectators is likely to be your partner or team-mate in a future match. This will make them paranoid that you will be pulling a face at them behind their back in a few weeks' time.

PICKING PLAYERS UP

Players may have given their all in the first set in a match and may still have lost and it is up to you, as captain, to get over to them the message that they may have lost a battle but they can still win the war. Much as we would all like to be able to come out with a Churchillian speech, it is more sensible to let the players recover a little from their defeat and then, as mentioned before, make a very small number of comments that focus on the positives of the situation and steer their minds onto the forthcoming rubber and away from the last rubber. If, for example, you are aware of their next opponent's weaknesses then mentioning this is a good route to go down as it is a good focus change.

PREPARATION – A MOTIVATIONAL FACTOR

A small but nevertheless important factor is the effect your preparation and organisational skills have on your own team members. The standard of your preparation can have a positive or negative motivational effect on them. Unfortunately being completely organised can be considered as a given by your team-mates and to some may not provide any individual motivational benefit. However some will see the work you put in and will appreciate it and will try that bit harder for you.

On the flip side, however, if you as captain are always late or are not sure whether one of your players is going to turn up or are continually forgetting scorecards, tennis balls etc. then this is soon going to grate on your players' nerves. Providing players with plenty of notice for a match and not asking them at the last minute is also an important point as it means they do not feel they are a last minute substitute.

Preparation is paramount, your team members will see good preparation and have increased confidence in you.

If there are a large number of tasks that need to be done in readiness for a match then ask your regular players to contribute and delegate some tasks to them. Don't be afraid to ask the regular members and even your key player(s) to carry out a particular task each time. Try to get them into a routine so, for example, if one person arrives early ask them to get the chairs out and measure the nets each week. This increased involvement in the team subconsciously increases their loyalty to the team and their will for the team to succeed.

USING GUILT TO MOTIVATE

We have discussed the power and effect that the captain's words can have. It should be noted that these words may not always work on a conscious level but could work on the players' subconscious level. I have had players who are due to play for me in a match on a Sunday morning. They are young players and I am fully aware that they will be going out on the Saturday night before, will get drunk and will turn up hung-over for the match. There is little I can do to stop them doing this and indeed why would I want to, I am not about to spoil anyone's fun. The only tactic I can use is damage limitation. I usually grin at them and tell them to get an early night before the match knowing full well they won't. However, we need to examine what happens at the subconscious level. The first entry that goes into the player's subconscious is that this match means a lot to their captain so when the inevitable hangover comes there is more likelihood of the player covering it up, not using it as an excuse (so not talking negatively) and doing their best due to feeling guilty.

RELAX THE OPPOSITION

One of my favourite psychological wins was something I did quite a time ago. It was a straight fight for the title between ourselves and one other team and we were playing the championship decider at their home venue. The match format was that each of our three pairs played twelve games against each of the opponent's three pairs resulting in 108 games being played in total. After the first round we were 24-12 down which was quite a deficit. Before the next round commenced, I went over to the opposition and out of earshot of my own team I said to all of them that they pretty much had this match wrapped up and that it was effectively over. One of their players looked at me and said that I didn't look like a player that would give up. I shrugged and walked off.

I then sat with my team and made them aware of what we needed to try and achieve, that it was still possible to win the match and talked through with them the kind of scores we needed to get back on track. In the end we pulled off a remarkable 56-52 win and won the title. Since then, I wondered whether what I said had any effect at all in effectively relaxing the opposition's minds.

Not so long ago I was playing pool and I had a fairly straightforward shot on the black to win the game. My opponent commented, "well you're not going miss that" and started putting his queue away in the rack. Sure enough I missed it by quite a distance purely due to the words that had come out of his mouth. From this I deduced that it was highly likely that what I had said in the tennis match did indeed have an effect. This also fits in to the same logic as the person who comments on his opponent's forehand working really well, just before the point where his opponent can't hit a forehand in the court to save his life. This is a useful tactic therefore that you could employ when you are next down in a crucial match.

PARTNERSHIP MOTIVATION

The key factor about a partnership is that you get on well. If you don't then you need to find another partner. Assuming you do get on well with your partner then we need to consider how you can make the partnership even better. During my research I have read that 2-3 years is the maximum length of time a tennis partnership should be together before they get fed up with each other. This doesn't seem unreasonable but I believe it depends so much on the circumstances, the individuals' personalities and whether they are playing together non-stop. So as well as looking at how we can make a partnership better we are also hoping to extend the longevity of team partnerships.

In Peter Scholl's book 'How to succeed at Tennis' he provides advice on choosing a partner, "Your views on tennis in general and on doubles in particular should coincide. You must believe in your partner's ability"

Partnerships very much reflect normal life. Let's look at mixed tennis as an example. In a mixed pairing if the gentleman acts as a gentleman then things are usually going to run a lot smoother. So generally good etiquette such as waiting to allow the lady to pass to the opposite side of the court first is going to help. Other niceties are recommended though. For example if your partner didn't bring a bottle of water the first time you played together then for your second match together buy two bottles of water and tell her you bought one for her. If your partner has a good feeling then it will be reflected in her tennis, she will enjoy it more, will relax more and play better. Jamie Murray's game plan for the 2007 mixed doubles at Wimbledon was 'Keep the lady happy'. This was concocted by Louis Cayer one of the world's leading experts on doubles. Jamie Murray went on to win the tournament with Jelena Jankovic.

A while ago my partner and I were playing against a couple where the server had been passed three tennis balls. As the server didn't have enough room in his pocket for the third tennis ball he passed it to his partner at the net to hold onto. This happened a number of times during the match and regardless of which of the opposition lady or gentleman was at the net, the net player always turned round to offer to pocket the third ball in order to help his partner out. What struck me at the time was not only the courtesy of the gesture and usefulness of it but the fact that this pair I was playing against seemed because of it, a real partnership, that they must have been playing together a long time and got on well. In my eyes I viewed them as being stronger then I had viewed them before they did this simple act for each other. Ever since that match I have always held the third tennis ball for my partner and vice versa as logic dictated that some of our opponents would think the same way as me.

Depending on the playfulness of your partner and if that person has a sense of humour then use that to your advantage. My tennis partner and I often gently shoulder-barge each other when passing and then both apologise as though it was an accident. Another girl I partner knows how to get me back on track if I hit a bad shot or am getting a bit frustrated by saying 'Come on Lobley, pull your finger out' and then grins at me.

Why not also call the person you are playing with 'Partner'. So instead of 'good shot Katy' throw in the odd 'good shot partner' as well and shoot your partner a grin. This has the effect of making your partner feel that not only is this a partnership but that you want it to be a partnership. The last point is important because there is always insecurity on a tennis court when playing doubles because one of you is always going to feel weaker than the other.

What are the other ways to motivate your partner? These can be more subtle and depend on the individual so you may need to work these out for yourself. All I can do is provide an example. One of my tennis partners prefers to receive in the advantage court which I myself prefer too so I make it known that I prefer that side and then I concede ground and let her receive in the advantage court. In the same way that letting players have an involvement in picking the team means they have some onus on them to prove they were right, I believe my partner tends to play better because she feels a small amount of guilt at playing at the side that she thinks I like to play on and therefore tries harder and invariably plays better.

On the flipside of partnership motivation is partnership de-motivation. We have covered the shoulder slumping effect, the rage etc, but just as important are the words you say to your partner in encouragement. It is vital that you know what effect these words will have on your partner. I have learnt this to my cost when playing in the deciding set of one of my team's bigger matches with a partner who I had been playing with for a number of years and I assumed coped well with pressure. I said to him 'right this is the big one, this is what it's all about playing in the crucial set in front of an audience' as these words reflected my mood of excitement. My partner, from being a very good player throughout the whole match all of a sudden, couldn't actually get the ball in court. I have never seen anyone collapse in such a way before and I therefore resolved to find out before a big match what comments my future partners reacted both best and badly to.

Another player I played matches with advised me that the way to get the best out of him is if I say, "the game we are in has no relevance to the overall match score" as he knew that if there was no pressure he would play better. This information he gave me is vital and can of course be found out fairly early on in a partnership just by asking the question. I always made sure I played down the importance of a match in future for him.

Another thing to agree with your partner is that neither of you will apologise during the match should you miss a shot. Even having agreed this both players will usually end up apologising just out of natural habit. However the reason it should be avoided is so that players are not apologising after every shot they miss as this will increase their own guilt levels and lower their confidence levels and also will usually just wind their partner up.

Motivation can also be provided by leadership in the partnership. Scholl comments as follows, "Although each partner has equal rights, one should act as leader. The leader does not have to be the better player, but rather the more experienced one. In the long run a team in which both or neither want to lead will not be harmonious"

WHAT DO YOU KNOW ABOUT YOUR PARTNER?

Van Raalte and Silver-Bernstein came up with a number of questions that should be put to your doubles partner. I have added further ones that I believe should be covered. Finding out this information is a very sensible idea although sitting your partner down and going through each question could be awkward but it is worth trying, as the answers to some of the questions might not be what you are expecting. It is highly likely that some things you say on court will really wind up your partner or put him under added pressure at crucial moments. If you are made aware of these things then it can improve harmony in the doubles partnership and improve results. Here are the questions you ask and the possible answers your partner might give:-

What would you like me to do when you make a mistake?

- Ignore it, so no facial expressions, no eye contact, no comments at all.
- Try to play down the impact, for example saying 'no worries', 'close, unlucky', 'good idea'.
- Help me to laugh it off.
- Encourage me e.g. saying 'keep going', 'you're still a genius'.
- Move the focus away, for example by picking fault in the opponents' game, saying 'I've noticed the opponent is retreating when we come to the net'.
- Remind me to keep focused.

What would you like me to do when the pressure is on?

- Do and say nothing.
- Talk about something non-tennis related or not related to this particular match.
- Remind me to keep concentrating.
- Point out that it all hangs on this and everyone is watching.
- Remind me of my primary/scondary level of motivation for beating the opposition.
- Show a display of confidence by e.g. pointing out the weaknesses of the opposition.
- Advising or discussing what the battle plan should be for the next point

- Remind me to stay calm.

What would you like me to do when we are losing?

- Remind me to keep the ball in court.
- Tell me to just go for my shots.
- Try to be more positive and give some encouragement.
- Increase communication between us.
- Decrease communication.
- Lighten the mood.

How can I be a better partner?

- Keep your cool and stay motivated even if I make an error.
- Go for your shots no matter how I play.
- By not criticising me.
- By providing constructive criticism only.
- By coaching me throughout the match.
- By not coaching me.
- By not poaching too much or by poaching more and taking control of the match.

How can we be a better team?

- By having either more or less squad get-togethers.
- By getting rid of the trouble causers in the squad.
- By getting the pairings right.
- By improving the organisation of the team.
- More training/coaching sessions.
- Having more fun.

THREE-QUARTER SEASON BREAK

Often at clubs, team players will try to fit as many matches into their schedule as they can. Very often this can be a flawed philosophy from either a physical or psychological perspective or sometimes both.

From a psychological perspective, most players have a point where once they have played too many matches in a certain period of time their enthusiasm wanes. It is very difficult for any person to know the maximum number and frequency of matches that he can play in a period without losing interest. However trying to work this out and then utilising the information can be crucial as to whether a player enjoys his tennis season and also so he can maximise his success. Obviously an enthusiastic player is more likely to do better than one who is just going through the motions because he is fed up of playing so many matches. Have a think about what your ideal number of matches in a week and a month would be.

The second issue is physical. Playing five matches in five days might be possible when you are eighteen years of age but becomes increasingly hard as you age. As you get older, you start picking up injuries which then have a negative effect on your enjoyment of your tennis.

It is worth looking at the schedule of matches that your club has in the forthcoming season. If you are a strong player who the captain will want to play then discuss with the captain which matches you are needed for and which he can manage without you. If you are not one of the top players then try to find out how many matches you are likely to be playing this season. Each person is different but if you, for example, are a player who likes to play two matches every week then try to set your schedule so that it is as near this as possible. So if one week there are four matches then tell the captain you are only available for two.

One idea worth considering is to have a mid-season break or more precisely a break at about the three-quarter mark in the season. This can be as little as ten days without picking up a racket however it will give your body time to recover from any knocks you may have picked up and also give your body a rest in time for the final push to win the title or avoid relegation. The time away from the court may mean you miss playing and it could therefore renew your enthusiasm at just the right time. A break about three quarters of the way through the season is the optimum time to have a rest.

TITLE MENTALITY

In order to get your players into the mind-set of challenging for the title, firstly you need to have players who are hungry for success, are talented and also want to improve. The second step is to get the team winning as many matches as possible so the players are used to winning. The third part is to make it the norm that the team is challenging each year for titles and appearing in cup finals.

Title Mentality is one of the hardest things to achieve from scratch with a team but it is what separates the best captains. Once you have your team players in that mind -set you will start to find that matches against teams where it was sometimes doubtful whether you would win, you now win routinely and your own players start to doubt themselves less and less. They forget about their fears.

Once you have this mind-set in place it will run of its own accord as though on auto-pilot. The dream end-state as captain is actually to not have to say anything from a motivational standpoint because you know your team will die for the cause anyway. A useful guide is that if you end up with a team that will play in torrential rain and never use the weather as an excuse you know you have the required psychological commitment to go on and win the title.

HEARTS AND MINDS

Modern warfare is fought not just using aggression and forcefulness but also by adopting the 'hearts and minds' philosophy, particularly by the elite special forces. The idea behind this is to achieve your goal, namely to win, by putting good experiences into people's hearts and minds so that you can get what you want. With the special forces this involves building up relationships and trust within local communities they are policing. In tennis terms, this is about winning over the hearts and minds of your own players. Your aim is to make them enjoy their experience of playing in your team to the point where they love playing and give up a lot of other things they might do to play in the team. If you are able to involve them in the ways discussed earlier in the book (keeping them up to date with the team's progress, getting them to help out, asking their opinions etc.) then they will take the team's destiny into their hearts and will do everything they can to help the team succeed.

SUMMARY

Your goal as team captain should be to create the most successful team you possibly can. Your aim should be to develop a team that is better than the sum of its parts. Achieving this is a great accomplishment and is almost solely down to thought and psychology.

Getting players to play their best tennis for you is paramount. In Michael Chang's autobiography 'Holding Serve' he concludes, "Size and strength are not the determining factors in tennis – heart is".

A large amount of psychological theory has been discussed and we have also focused on the application of the theory by way of examples. However, it is only you as captain who is in the position to work out what is best for your players and yourself so that when it gets to the business end of the season, you and your team are still in the hunt for silverware. You know your players a lot better than I do, you just need to find out how their minds work and then think about how to get the best out of them.

8 GAMESMANSHIP

MATCH CALLS

One thing that has crept into tennis over the years is what is commonly referred to as 'match calls'. This is often joked about at social club time where a player may have accurately called a line-ball in but would then follow it up with a comment of 'had it been a match there is no way I would have called that in'. Effectively, what we are dealing with when a player calls a good ball out in a match, is cheating. This chapter is about gamesmanship but I want to make it clear that gamesmanship and cheating are two different things. The former is stretching the rules, the latter is breaking them. We should all be on our guard to make sure that match calls not only stop coming into the game but that they are removed from the game altogether. A ball is either in or out regardless of the circumstance. If you have been cheated but continue to be honest you will impress those watching, make your opponent feel guilty and may even stop him cheating.

The mind is a complex beast however and I am of the firm belief that some players want the ball to land out so badly that even when it has landed in they are genuinely convinced that it actually landed out. Jake Barnes in 'Social Tennis' recalls the behaviour of an elderly lady at his club, "Ellie it seems, takes the game far more intensely than the other players, and the consensus of opinion is that Ellie actually *sees* close balls as out". As we see now with video replay technology in professional tennis, the best players in the world often make bad calls (even on calls when they are making a genuine challenge rather than a hopeful one) although, to give them their due, their shots tend to be travelling a lot faster than the average club player's. Barnes summarises, "Tennis is a game of flash judgements".

The key thing to bear in mind is that you need to be honest in order to know how good you really are.

BEATING THE CHEAT TO THE CALL

If you are up against an opponent who you know is a bad caller then it's often useful to get your own call in first despite it not being your shout. If you or your partner hit a shot that you know to be a winner then the instant it lands, shout 'Good shot' and walk across the court to be in position for your next shot. This is a way of making it more difficult for the renowned bad caller at the other side of the net to call it out. If this technique is used against a dodgy caller then I think it is fair game as all you are doing is making sure you aren't going to be cheated. If it is being used against even good callers then we are into the realms of gamesmanship. If you are doing it when you know it to be out then we move into cheating.

EVENING THINGS UP

A friend I play with, who likes to make a stand against cheats, told me the story of how she sought parity after having had a bad call against her. She had hit a shot which landed inside the line and her opponent, a known bad caller, called it out. My friend was naturally upset but said nothing at all to her opponent. On the next point my friend served again and when the return came back and landed two metres inside the court, my friend called it out. Her opponent was in disbelief and said "that was miles in!". My friend just shook her head, gave no explanation or retort, and just said "Nope I saw that as out". As it was her call there was nothing at all her opponent could do about it. One thing did change though, the bad calling stopped. Although I am supposed to take the moral high ground at this point and say that one bad call shouldn't be met by another in return, it did takes guts to do what she did and not stand down. I'm not sure it's something that I would do though or recommend, but it sorted her opponent out.

HOME ADVANTAGE

Gamesmanship can take many forms and one of

these can relate to knowledge you have of your own courts and experience of playing on them. For example, if there is a lot less room at the back or at the sides of your courts compared to most courts then how about trying to get the ball at such an acute angle that it sends your opponent crashing into the netting that surrounds the courts. As you have experience of playing on your courts you may have perfected how to attain the required acute angle. One tip mentioned earlier is to get very near the net when volleying.

Sending an opponent crashing into the side netting can be a great challenge and in a sadistic way, quite good fun – definitely worth trying. No rules are being broken and it is a good way of improving your angled shot play. It is the opponent's choice if he wishes to risk life and limb – all you are doing is giving him the opportunity to do it. If you play in an away match where there is little room at the sides then watch out for your opponents doing the same to you and if you can why not try it to them.

Another common trick is if there isn't much room at the back of the court. This scenario makes the whipped topspin lob a supremely effective shot if both of your opponents are at the net. If this shot clears the players at the net then more often than not it will be deep enough to be almost irretrievable because although your opponents may be able to move faster than the speed the ball is moving, by the time the topspin has kicked in they will have run out of court before they can get it.

ENSURING YOUR OPPONENT HASN'T PRACTISED HIS SHOTS

A lot of players have a glaring weakness which you may remember from your last encounter or you may discover in the warm up. Most players are keen to keep this weakness covered up as best they can and some are only too happy to not hit the shot at all during the warm up as they want to try to keep it hidden. Usually it is glaringly obvious and my recommendation is that you give them exactly what they want. If you are able to warm up all but one of your opponent's shots, i.e. make sure he doesn't get to practice his weak shot and he is happy about this, then if you hit to this weakness in the match, this will virtually guarantee you winning the first few games. If it's obvious in the warm up however that your opponent wants to practice every shot then you should do so as its bad etiquette not to. That doesn't mean though that you can't favour hitting more balls to their strengths.

Should your opponent do this to you, let's say he hits every shot in the warm up to your forehand rather than your backhand then this gives you a great opportunity to work on your footwork and get yourself in position for a backhand. Not only does it warm up the shot your opponent doesn't want you warming up but you will get a sweat on too.

YOUR OPPONENT'S INJURIES

We have mentioned, in an earlier chapter, talking to the opponent about his injuries before or during the match and how he likes to use these injuries as an excuse when he is starting to lose points. I believe that if someone has had a very serious injury and is back playing again then discussing it just to give yourself an advantage is a little out of order. Throughout the course of your tennis career however you are likely to suffer all the same niggling injuries that everyone else suffers but it is how you handle them that makes the difference. If you say to yourself that you are never going to mention or show an injury, unless it's impossible not to of course, then no one will know that you have an injury or weakness. If your opponent is happy to talk to you about his injuries though, it increases the likelihood that he will be thinking about his injuries whilst hitting his shots, which will seriously hamper his chances.

RACKET THROWING

As a seasoned campaigner, one of the unwritten rules is to do everything in your power to get your opponent to throw a tantrum. The ultimate, of course, is seeing his racket being flung across the court and how often do we see this from juniors. If someone is about to explode then it would be rude of you not to assist by ensuring he loses the next point after a strop. The key when he is about to lose the plot is to keep the ball in the court. If he is a hard hitter who likes to play against opponents who play tennis in what he deems to be the 'correct' style, then throw in a few slow balls and lobs to annoy him. For the veteran campaigner there can be great satisfaction in getting an opponent to throw his racket.

This latter game plan of slowing the game down and throwing in lobs to infuriate your opponent is a good tactic if you need a Plan B due to your Plan A not working. Some players, as part of their normal game, make a living out of frustrating opponents. John McEnroe commented on Brad Gilbert's style, "The style of play reflected his personality: He'd bring you down, and suck your energy dry."

THE COMPLIMENT

If a player is playing unusually well and in particular one of his shots is on song, then it is highly likely that he is not really thinking too much about what he is doing and is just swinging away. One of the most well known psychological tips for throwing a player off his rhythm is to compliment him on how well that particular shot is playing at the moment. You can often learn the effect of this before he even hits his next shot as he will commonly say, "don't say that – I won't be able to hit one in now" and sure enough, he starts thinking too hard about the shot and starts missing it. Personally, I feel this is a sneaky bit of gamesmanship and try not to use it, unless I'm in a bad situation when anything within the rules goes. Another one of course is the exclamation of, "Don't you ever double fault?" just as he has boomed a service down passed you although this is pushing it a little as it is blindingly obvious you are using dirty tactics. Beware of doing this to a strong player though, as he is usually more astute. He will see it as a great challenge to prove that you are unable to psych him out and will therefore step up a gear and make sure he doesn't miss a shot.

9 THE OPPOSITION

THE RECEIVER'S RETURNS

Allen Fox advises that the position of the server's partner at the net should be based on the types of shots that the opposition receiver tends to play, "The net player should adjust his position depending on the proclivities of the receiver. If you find the receiver never lobs, move in closer to the net. If the receiver never hits down the line, move closer to the centre of the court to reduce the area in which he dares to hit. Some players always position themselves in the same place at the net, no matter what the receivers do. This is a mistake. Be aware of the receiver's capabilities and adjust accordingly."

THE TENNIS COACH

A phrase I have heard many times in the past is, "This guy we're about to play is a tennis coach" and you can hear the fear and trepidation in the person's voice who is saying it. In actual fact, many coaches are not great match players. Let's consider the facts. If he is a good coach then he is likely to be on court doing a physical job forty hours a week and having coached for eight hours in a day, he is hardly going to be in peak physical shape to play a three hour match or indeed be in the best mental state for it as he may well have had enough of tennis courts and tennis players for one day. In my experience, I have sometimes found coaches to be tired and not actually wanting to play a match.

A second point to consider is that the majority of tennis coaching does not involve hitting the ball hard. In fact, most of the time, it is about feeding balls to beginners all day long. I have had a coach say to me that he finds it very difficult switching from feeding players all day long to doing exactly the opposite, i.e. keeping the ball away from his opponent when it comes to a match. The coach in question said that it often took him a number of games before he got into the match.

A third point is, that coaches do not as a rule play anything like the same number of matches as normal team players play due to the fact that they are usually paid by the hour so need to be earning rather than playing matches. This means they are not as match-tight when they do get round to playing a match.

You should also bear in mind that a lot of coaches have a great style of play however their consistency in a match is not always there. So in summary, not only should you not be afraid of the coach you are about to play against in a match but should look upon it as a great chance to get a win. Always learn to play the court, not the name on the other side of the net.

THE OPPONENT WHO HAS DONE IT ALL

People often like to talk about the greatest sporting achievement in their life. For example, if I were to tell you mine it would be that I have beaten a player in a singles tournament who has beaten Tim Henman. I tend then however to explain the situation a little more fully, namely that the player I beat who was in his mid-twenties at the time when I played him, played Tim Henman when Henman was only eleven and my opponent was fourteen. So I'm not totally sure it's something I can be that proud of but it's a story nevertheless. Most people have a story of this type, be it a player winning the Warwickshire under-14 doubles title fifty years ago or them beating a county player last week. The timing of people telling you these stories can be significant though.

I recently entered a regional doubles tournament and my partner and I got through the group stages and qualified for the semi-final of the tournament where we faced the coach of another one of the big clubs in the area. Before the match, the rather garrulous coach told us a little story of how he had recently played the number one in the world at a sport which involved playing tennis, badminton and table tennis where the players add up the points they earned in each sport in order to get a grand total. His throwaway last sentence was then that he had beaten the number one in the world at the tennis part of the three matches.

My partner and I managed to win the match and

progressed to the final where we faced another coach who was the coach of the club which was hosting the event. However, I had never come across this player before so how did I know he was a coach? Well it is quite simple, he deliberately made an effort to talk to me before the final and tell me that he was the coach at the club as well as the coach at another big club. So my question to you here is, whether you can see a pattern emerging?

Why do these players need to say such things? Well clearly, it is to try to intimidate you. In fact though, that is just the outer layer. If you remove the outer layer they are actually very fearful underneath. After all, here they are, in this case coaches, worried about their reputation. They are under a huge amount of pressure as they are desperate to win so that their customers will want to be taught by the regional champion. They have everything to lose and nothing to gain. The best they can do is to break-even by winning the tournament which is what their customers would expect them to do. So any time in the future you hear an opponent who you are about to step on court with, regaling you with stories of how he was hitting with the number five in the country last weekend, then think to yourself that the only reason this person is going out of his way to tell you this story is because he is wary of playing you.

BAD DAY AT THE OFFICE

If your preparation is good before a match, you arrive in plenty of time and you can get to partner a player who you get on well with, then you are more likely to be going into the match in a positive frame of mind, than if any of these were not the case. These are typical examples of things that you have control of and can make sure happen. If you are coming into the match with this positive relaxed mindset then it is impossible for your opponent to be in a better frame of mind with regard to the points mentioned.

A great number of people who you come across in life try to cram too many activities into too short a time period. I'm sure you know the type, those who come charging onto the court apologising for being late and all in a fluster. There are also the type of people where everything is negative, they've had a terrible day at work, they're injured, they don't want to play with the partner they've been put with and so on. Then, of course, there are circumstances where your opponent may have had a row with his other half before the match or may be feeling unwell.

So logically, your opponent can be one of two things, either he is in a good place and so neither you nor your opponent has an edge over the other or he can be in a bad place thus handing you an immediate advantage.

This is a good way of giving yourself a small reassurance boost if you are in a good frame of mind. Think about all the possible things that your opponent could be worrying about and think to yourself that at best your opponent can only have as good a mindset as you and more likely than not he is in a worse state of mind.

FORGETTING YOUR OWN WEAKNESSES AND CONCENTRATING ON THE OPPOSITION'S

When interviewing a lot of club players, the most common issues raised are fear of their own weaknesses and also their opponent's strengths. If you are one of the many players who have these thoughts then what we are going to do is to try and reverse this mindset.

In order to become more successful, you need to apply some basic logic. You might be fully aware of your own weaknesses but your opponent is unlikely to know about them and indeed may not believe you to have any. Even when he does work out your weaknesses, it might be very late on in a match when it is already beyond your opponent's grasp. The reason a player doesn't often work out his opponent's weaknesses is because a lot of players do not put too much thought into their plan of attack, they are primarily concerned with their own game to the point of ignoring everything else.

In an earlier chapter, we covered the following logic 'because the player you are facing has not played at Wimbledon then he must have weaknesses'. Think about this for a moment. You now need to allocate the time that you used to spend worrying about your own weaknesses into working out your opponent's weaknesses. Treat it as a straight swap.

As most players do worry when they go on court, it is safe to assume that your opponent is worried. Let us assume here that you have managed to free yourself of any of your concerns by considering the points made in the previous paragraphs.

Having spent time working out your opponent's weaknesses then put yourself in his head for a moment and think about the issues he has in his mind about how he is going to cover up his weaknesses against you. You know he has a weak backhand when put under pressure and both you and he know that you know this and that you are going to play on it. By putting yourself in your opponent's mind you can quite easily see the problems he is going to have. This is not looking good for him.

So let's see where your opponent's mindset is before he starts the match against you. He is coming on court to play an excellent player (you) who is well prepared and psychologically in a good place. Your opponent is likely to be worried as that is the natural human instinct of the tennis player. Also you are now sympathising with his predicament because you are about to expose his weaknesses. So as well as him being worried about his plight, you are worried for him too. That's a whole lot of worry all on one side of the court! Fortunately, it's on your opponent's side.

Another way of dealing with worries common to both you and your opponent on match day, for example, slippy courts, bad weather etc., is to have the mindset that the negative thoughts which are in your head are actually not yours but the thoughts in your opponent's head. So when you have a bad thought – turn it round.

USING HATE

Each person's mind works differently, however a lot of players find that if they hate their opponent or the opponent has done something that has really wound them up, then they can play better against them than they would normally. It's a combination of adrenalin rush and hugely increased concentration and focus.

McEnroe states in Borg v McEnroe (2005), "I had to go out there knowing I could feel I wanted to kill the other guy. Everything becomes personal. To me, when I look back, that's the beauty of it. That's the fun."

So if you are playing a crucial match but have no malice for your opponent is it possible to kid your mind into thinking you have? Without showing it to your opponent, is it possible to use a small thing they've done such as a facial expression or an over-confident comment to give you that little bit extra?

Hate is a weapon I use occasionally in my game and I ensure it is channelled into playing effectively. However there was one occasion where the hate I had in my head for a future opponent dissipated and it ended up costing me. I was playing in an internal tennis tournament at a big club when I was young and I was determined to play the club number one as he was so arrogant I wanted to try and beat him. I was in the opposite half of the draw to him and in the semi-finals I beat a player who I wasn't expected to beat. After the match, the club number one came up to me and started treating me as an equal, he was civil, polite and a nice guy, a total contrast to the arrogant person I had seen before. So all of a sudden the arrogance had gone but because of this what had also gone was my primary motivation against him. Having had him speak to me in the way he did, the hate I had for him had been taken away and in the end so were my chances of beating him. He was a far stronger player than me and would have won the match anyway but him removing the hate factor was an interesting psychological lesson that I learnt, although to this day I have no idea whether he was aware of the effect he had had just by talking to me in a reasonable way. He was probably unaware that I disliked him so much, so it is unlikely it was deliberate on his part. It was more likely to have been just circumstance. In the final though, having had my primary motivation taken away from me, I was unable to replace the hate with some other form of motivation so there was a huge hole in my psychological makeup which made the score line that much worse!

ONE SHOT WONDER

Let us say that you play a shot which pushes your opponent way out of court, you have narrowed the angle and the situation is looking good. Your opponent then unleashes a mighty drive down your line for a glorious winner. Having had this done to you once, the usual reaction from a lot of players is to avoid playing the same shot again, i.e. you avoid sending the player out wide because you assume that your opponent can pull this shot out of the bag every time, clearly ignoring what you actually know, namely that it is a low percentage shot that your opponent would surely not be able to pull off time and time again. Just because your opponent hits one great shot, never assume he can hit the same great shot twice. Well this is great in theory but is it correct? Well you won't know until you try it. After you have lost a point to a glorious winner but you know that the position you are taking up is technically, logically and geometrically correct to give you the maximum mathematical possibility of winning the point, then try it again. It is highly likely that you will find your opponent is not only incapable of hitting the same winner each time but that you can win a lot of points from an area of his game that you might initially have thought was his strength.

HANDING OUT INCORRECT INFORMATION

One year at the league's AGM which took place a long time before the season started, I was talking to the captain of our main rivals for the league title. It was my first year of running this particular team and I had some strong players at my disposal including one girl who played for Scotland at the time and another who was number one in her county. The opposition captain asked me how I was going to play it this year as he knew I had a huge squad of players to choose from.

I fed him the line that I wanted to try and give everyone a chance to play in the team and that it wasn't just the best players who would play every week as I wanted to make it fair for everyone and I wasn't as results orientated as the previous captain. He took this information away with him.

We played his team fairly early on in the season and I fielded an all-star cast for the match as I always tried to do for every match. When we arrived for the match it was clear that the opposition captain hadn't picked his team based on us turning out such a strong side. As the match wore on I watched him visibly drowning as he tried to keep his team above water. At the end of it he said to me, "I thought you weren't putting out all your best players!" I could only grin and say "Sorry buddy, I lied".

This tactic can only be used once against each opposition captain, however in this scenario it gave us a great springboard for our title winning season.

YOUR OPPONENT'S WEAKNESSES

In doubles it is always easier to learn about a player's weaknesses when you are partnering him than when you are playing against him. This is because when playing with a partner your pattern recognition is enhanced so if he were to miss two identical shots in a row the normal thought to have is that this is your partners glaring weakness. If the player was at the other side of the court and missed the same two shots your natural reaction is to notice he has missed them but not to necessarily link this with being the player's weakness.

In order to find a player's weaknesses therefore you will learn these quicker and will remember them better if you play with him rather than against him. Naturally, this is not possible in a league situation as you are always playing against the player. There is a way to do it though, and that is by asking an opposition player to enter a tournament with you. That way you get to partner him, learn his weaknesses and then you can use this information against him in future matches. You may also enjoy getting to play with him in a tournament as well of course.

DON'T WIND UP THE SUPERSTAR

Every now and again you will come up against a player who is far better and stronger than anyone else you normally come across. This type of player is usually fairly laid back and he wants to wander about the court and win the match without really trying. He often has no great motivation for the match as he finds it all too easy. When you are playing such a player, in order to win as many games against him as possible, it is important that you keep him in this relaxed mode. In fact, if you are able to have a laugh and joke with him between changeovers, then you can actually relax him further to the point that it doesn't bother him to lose the odd point or two to you as he likes you. If it's possible for you to maintain the joviality whilst actually trying your hardest, without making it look like you are, then you will be surprised at how many games you can win.

The opposite of this though can be a disaster. As mentioned, the superstar player may not be that motivated for the game so you need to make sure you don't give him a reason to be motivated (this would be a secondary level of motivation). The most common example that I have seen, is when a player tries ridiculously hard to beat the superstar and gets angry and acts like a bit of a fool. This effectively provides the superstar with a motivational tool, namely that he wants to humiliate this guy as it will give him pleasure to make him even angrier. The superstar will suddenly increase his focus and concentration and this will possibly last for the whole match which means if it's a team match then he will want to win the match too and it will therefore affect the games against the other pairs.

It is sensible therefore to keep the superstar passive and make it seem that the match is only a friendly, whilst doing everything in your power to win each point.

THE OPPONENT WHO BELIEVES HE IS BETTER THAN HE IS

Occasionally you will come across players who have already decided what they should achieve in their upcoming match against each of the opposing pairs. We had a match against such a player a number of years ago. On our team there was little difference between our first and third pairs. Our first pair had not arrived for the start of the match so our third pair instead played straight away against the opponent who I mentioned earlier who had preconceived ideas of what scores he should get against each pair.

The opponent in question and his partner, were their number one pair and he knew that he was playing what was effectively our third pair in this first set and expected to comfortably dispatch our thirds and get the match off to a good start for his team. I even believe that he had a preconceived score line in his head of what was acceptable for him and his partner to win by. In a 12-game set though they ended up losing 7-5 to our thirds and following that he collapsed spectacularly. The gentleman in question completely lost his head and ended up losing 12-0 against our seconds and basically handed the whole match to us.

It is quite rare to have an occurrence like this (although it is more common with juniors) and it is difficult to tactically 'cause' this reaction in an opponent other than by always trying to win against him.

What it does highlight however is how important it is to not necessarily set yourself exact score line goals on what you 'must' achieve. You can't always predict every part of a tennis match, for example, an opponent may have improved or got worse since last time or he might have a good day or an off day. The main thing is to try to focus on how to win the next point and not let your mind drift ahead to what score you expect to get.

THE 3D PLAYER PROFILE

This concept is best explained by focusing on singles. Once you understand the way it is applied in singles you can try to apply it to doubles. What we are doing here is putting our visual imagery down on paper. We split the opponent's side of the court into different sections and then assess his strength in each of those sections. We give each section a rating of white, grey or black where white means it is a part of the court where your opponent is not going to trouble you from and black means a place on the court where if you put the ball there it is likely your opponent is going to hit an outright winner. Grey is obviously a mid-point and this means it is not an area we are as concerned with focusing on.

If we analyse your opponent's side of the court then

we can split it up into quadrants, namely, your opponent's backhand when he stands on the baseline, his forehand when he is on the baseline and then his backhand and forehand sides when he is at the net (conveniently these are the two service boxes as well).

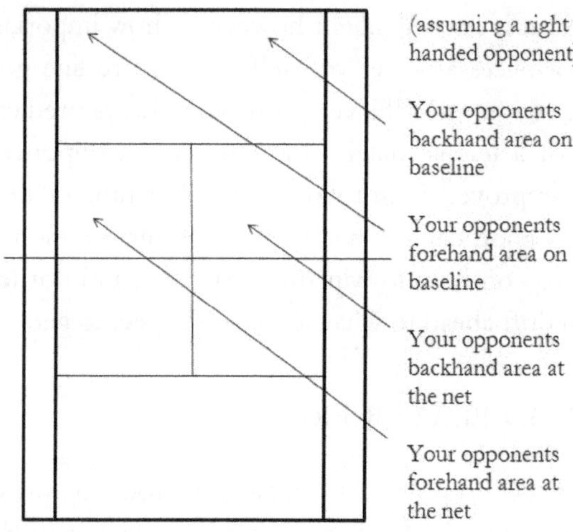

This can also be viewed in 3-D as shown below:

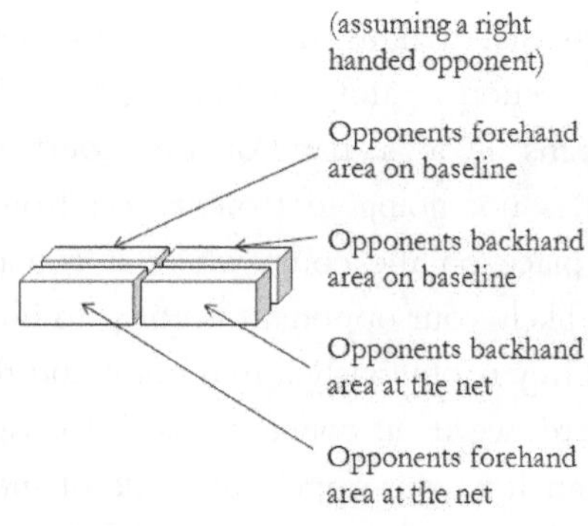

At this point the diagram is of little help because the height of the ball when your opponent is about to strike it has not been taken into account. We therefore need to continue building our 3-D view. As the ball can be hit by your opponent when it is down at his feet, at waist height or as an overhead then we need 3 layers.

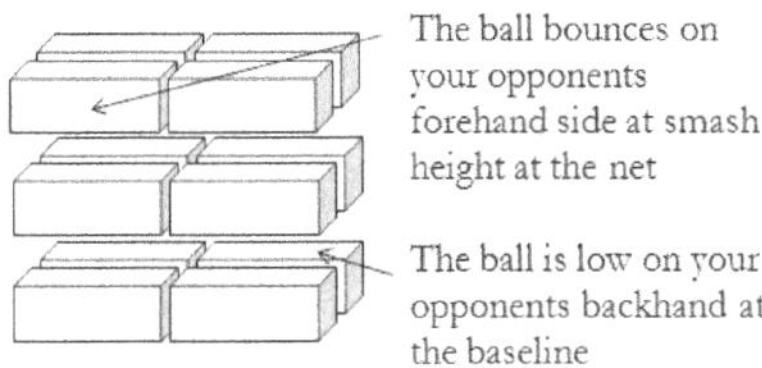
The ball bounces on your opponents forehand side at smash height at the net
The ball is low on your opponents backhand at the baseline

So having split your opponent's court into twelve sections you now need to analyse your opponent's game and then colour each box accordingly in white (safe for you), grey (neutral) or black (danger for you).

For one of my opponents, I know he has the following strengths and weakness:-

Strengths:

- Backhand from the baseline at waist height.
- Forehand waist height at the net.

Weakness:

- Low at either side when at the net.
- High kicking shot at the baseline on both sides

My diagram for this opponent would therefore be as follows:

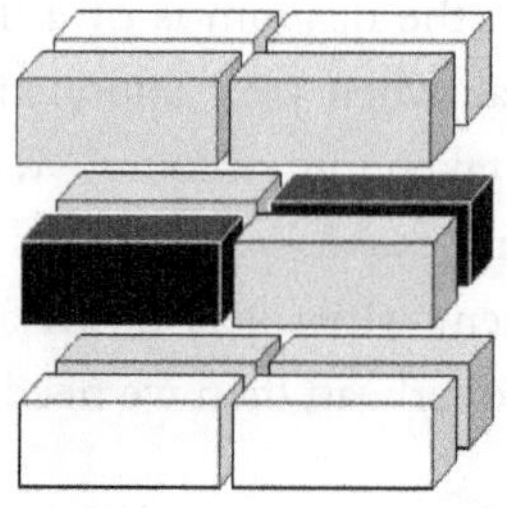

In the example above you will notice that I have not included as black (danger) sections some which you would expect, such as when the ball bounces at waist height on the backhand side at the net. The reason these are not black (danger) for this particular opponent is because on the backhand side when my opponent approaches the net, I know he will not change from his double handed backhand grip and therefore his shoulder rotation when on the run is severely limited. So he does not then generate as much power as he can from the baseline, where he would have had chance to prepare for his shot. This means that with this particular opponent there is no great danger in this area so it is not a bad place to hit the ball to if I get into trouble and can't get the ball to one of my recognised white (safe) areas. Of course with a different opponent who has a great backhand slice volley it would be a black section here.

The diagram created here is made up from the visual images of the opponent playing the shot he makes in each section of the 3-D court. So by you carrying out this exercise, the information in your mind has been drawn out on a piece of paper or a computer screen, so that it is possible to break down the whole of the opponents game. Effectively it displays the blueprint of the opponent's game. The next stage then is to project the diagram which is on paper back into your mind as a visual image. So you are effectively taking a photograph of the diagram, visualising where the safe and danger areas are, in the hope that when you are trying to dig out a return from a difficult situation, you can play the ball back to the safest area possible against this particular opponent.

One great benefit of this also is that you are spending time evaluating your opponent's whole game before playing them which will provide you with a great advantage.

10 COACHING

AFFORDABLE COACHING

Whatever age you are and no matter what the sport, it is always worth getting coaching. A typical reason for people electing not to get coaching is their perception of the cost, "I can't afford £20 or £30 an hour". However, why not ask friends or other members of the club to see if anyone else would be interested in getting coaching as well. If £20 is split between four players, £5 is quite cheap for one hour's work with a professional. Although one-to-one coaching is always going to be better than one-to-many, the difference between one-to-one and one-to-four is not significant. It only becomes less effective if there are five or more involved. Even then it is better than not having coaching at all.

If cost is still an issue, then think about how else coaching might be achieved. Some clubs hire a coach once a week or once a fortnight in the summer to coach everyone who turns up to the specifically organized coaching session and this is covered by part of the annual membership fee. If your club doesn't already do this, then why not suggest it at the next AGM. If this is met with resistance due to the cost then suggest that the coaching cost is covered by increasing the annual subscription by 5%. Improving the overall standard of tennis play at the club is always a good aim to have.

COACHING BY WATCHING PROFESSIONALS - RECORDING, REPEATING AND PRETENCE

Free coaching is also available and this is provided in your own living room. Watch the best professional players on television and see how they play their shots. If you have access to a sports channel which shows tennis then watch how the top players hit a backhand topspin for example and copy the movement. If you don't have access to a channel showing tennis then go onto youtube and watch Roger Federer or Justine Henin hit a backhand. Alternatively, the next time tennis is on, for example, when Wimbledon is shown then record the players playing and keep the recording. The importance of visualisation in improving your tennis cannot be understated, you will come to realise how useful it can be to have a recording saved to refer to at any time of the year.

The key to learning from watching the professionals play, is not so much to focus on each detail but on the whole cycle of a particular shot. If you were to watch each detail then you could break it down into many different areas, for example, if the player is serving then the analysis might begin as follows:-

- Where is his starting position?
- Where do his feet move?
- How high is the ball thrown?
- How far forward is it thrown?
- How far to the right is it thrown?

The list could go on and on. The advantage of the human mind however is that if there are a hundred individual details then the mind will record almost all of these sub-consciously even though consciously you may only be able to recall a very small number of them. This is a great positive as it means that each time you are watching the best players in the world play their shots then it gives you more chance to be able to replicate the style that they use.

When watching the professional player therefore let your mind 'record' the whole cycle of the shot from the moment the player begins his motion up to the point when he is moving his body to prepare for the next shot. If you have a mirror in the same room as the television then repeat the whole shot cycle simulating just what the professional has done without thinking about any of the details. Then 'record' how you have played the stroke in the mirror and then watch the professional again. It is entirely possible to have an identical technique as the professional, there is nothing stopping you achieving this. Keep repeating the recording and viewing process until your technique is identical. If you have a large room and a high ceiling then you could simulate the shot using a tennis racket.

Think about the logic behind doing this exercise. If you are replicating the motion of the best in the world and can take that out onto the practice court with you then you are giving yourself a lot better chance of playing a correct shot than if you were trying to play the shot with no help at all. Don't underestimate watching television as a great way to learn how to play the game correctly.

Another useful thing to watch is certain players manner on court. When Roger Federer is zeroing in on the net, knowing his opponent has given him a volley which is an easy put away, he may choose to slice an attacking backhand volley downwards. As he does this he will often have his chest puffed out with an air of arrogance and the manner in which he chops the ball down is almost one of disdain. This way of hitting the ball however is not to be confused with the nature of the player himself. These mannerisms and ways of playing the shot are massively important in the results that Federer gets. The footwork, determination and work rate needs to be there of course but also an arrogance and confidence at the moment of playing the shot and built into the shot can make a significant difference.

Youtube is also a fantastic place to improve your tennis. There are many coaching videos from professionals covering the technique of each shot in the game. Watch their videos, practice in front of the mirror and then take the technique out onto the practice court with you.

So where is this leading? Well, it is leading to pretence. Pretence is the next concept you need to master in order to improve technique. Having learnt how to carry out the motion of the shot, go on the court pretending that you are the player that you have been watching. Rather than thinking this is foolish or immature, it is actually a great way of boosting your confidence which in tennis is key. After all no one has any idea that you are pretending to be a player you have watched on television. Just relax and repeat the motion you have been practising. Embrace the confidence and arrogance (this is 'good' arrogance) of the tennis coach or professional and recreate it in yourself and your motion.

If you are keen enough then use or borrow a camcorder and video yourself playing tennis and compare it with the professionals; look at the differences and see what you are doing wrong. If you have the technology then you can even take the camcorder to the club with your friends and also a laptop and watch your play with your friends after the match and review each other's shots. Alternatively video each other playing shots on your phones and play them back.

There is also a way of being able to watch yourself playing a shot as you are actually playing it. It is undoubtedly a method you will not have thought of but does work very well. Depending on the time of day and year and providing the sun is shining, you can play a shot and using your peripheral vision see the motion you are making by watching your shadow. Now the key lesson we are taught when learning the game is of course to keep your eye on the ball, however if you are just practising there is no harm in giving this a try – it is a surprisingly clever technique to use. Depending on where you are standing and the position of the sun then your shadow can of course be elongated and stretched out before you, making it easier to see. Try watching your style in your shadow and see if it looks technically correct or not.

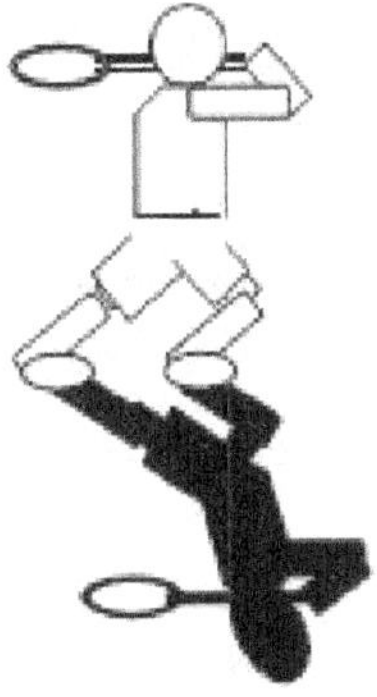

Fig 14 Using peripheral vision

A number of cities in Britain host 'satellite' or 'futures' tournaments for players who play at the level below the main professional ATP tour. To the local club player the standard of play at these tournaments is mind blowing and is definitely worth seeing. Watch out for when these tournaments are on and if you have some spare time, go along and see them in action and learn from the way they play. Another place where it's possible to see top players playing is at the sport orientated universities. If you happen to live near one of these universities, such as Loughborough or Leeds Carnegie, then find out when their first team train and go down and watch them play.

THE BENEFITS OF COACHING

We had a team player at our club who was trying hard to perfect a topspin backhand. I was watching from the sidelines and although his style looked fairly good he was struggling to hit two backhands in a row into the court. I called him over and looked at how he was holding the racket. He needed to move his hand round the handle grip by only two millimetres. He tried it again and hit twenty consecutive backhands into court. This is a classic example of the benefit of coaching. He had everything right bar a minor technicality.

When I was young I watched a player at our club who had a superb backhand topspin and I asked him how he managed to get such a consistent shot because up to this point I had only ever had a slice backhand. He advised of the two step process, firstly learning how to hit the stroke technically correctly and secondly playing for an entire season without ever running round his backhand and making sure he did not hit a slice unless there was no other option. After playing for a full season in this way he discovered he had perfected the backhand topspin. I had to try this. At any opportunity we would do drills just hitting backhand to backhand non-stop, before long it become routine and it is incredible how much power can be unleashed just by the correct technique, timing and belief. A year later after hitting only topspin backhands and no sliced backhands, I had a superb backhand topspin and like riding a bike it never goes away.

DOES YOUR COACH KNOW HOW TO PLAY TENNIS?

Much speculation is made about why Britain produces so few top tennis players. The main reason for this is the quality of coaching throughout the country. This is certainly not to say that every coach in the country is poor – you need to be able to spot the difference between a good coach and a bad one so that you can get the right one. I will try to help you do this.

I had a conversation with a friend of mine who had recently become a qualified coach and he said how great it was that anyone who can pick up a racket in Britain can become a tennis coach. My response however was exactly the contrary – this isn't a good thing – this is the actual problem! People who can't play tennis themselves are teaching others, including children, incorrectly. A child looks up to his coach just as he does to his parents, he imitates the coach's actions and wants to be just like him. Where there is one bad coach there is the potential for hundreds of poor players and the risk of you wasting your time, wasting your money, making you a poorer player for the rest of your life and potentially therefore putting you off one of the most wonderful games.

We have all heard it said that the best coaches were not always the best players. Michael Chang was coached by his brother Carl who never played on the professional tour. However he still played tennis to a very good standard, was a great student of the game and was able to put the time into analysing his brother's game as well as the opponents. In the same way at your local club the coach may not be the best player however the key point is that he must be able to play the game technically correctly, as well as being a good teacher of course.

I have had coaching from a poor coach when I was young and an exceptional coach at a later stage. It goes without saying that the latter was an inspiration. He was a good county standard player and a pleasure to watch playing and I learnt a great deal. The former coach however was a club player who was not even at my standard when I was fourteen. I recall he spent fifty minutes of the one hour lesson teaching myself and fifteen other kids how to hold the racket! Fifty minutes! Scarcely believable but needless to say after four lessons I stopped going to the coaching sessions. It was only later that I realised he had been teaching us the wrong way to hold the racket.

Stand on the sidelines and watch the coach in action in a match and see if he plays in the same style as you see the professionals play when you watch them. Don't take it for granted that each coach is a good one.

If you are tasked with bringing in a new coach for your club then start by asking the best coach in the region, try and twist his arm to free up a couple of hours. Only if the best continues to say no should you move down the list. The best coach is the one who is not only a good coach but who is also held in awe by his students. Students who look at their coach in awe will be better listeners, better learners and keener, three of the key attributes any pupil should have. One good coach, can bring through a great crop of youngsters. Once the youngsters have the love of the club in their hearts then it often stays with them through adulthood and a club can be sustained or sustain a very high level just through one good group of youngsters.

A vital contribution that your club coach should be making is to be pro-active and go into the local schools and bring the kids down to the club and start the whole coaching process from the beginning. If your club coach isn't doing this then ask him if this is something he would consider. If he won't then look at getting another coach who will do this, possibly working alongside the original coach.

THE EFFECT OF COACHING

The effect of the absence of coaching when starting out is not often realised by the player until a lot later on in the tennis players life; sometimes this can be years later. Players often start playing tennis without getting coaching. Later on they see the better players at the club playing in a particular style and want to emulate them. Often by this time their bad habits and poor style are so ingrained it would almost be a case of scrapping everything and going back to the drawing board. That is easier said than done though.

Compare this with a child or someone who has never played before, they are actually a lot better prospect as the coach can begin with a blank canvas. This is not to say that coaching cannot improve your technique and play, of course it can, but what this example shows is that the sooner you get coaching, the better.

A good analogy is the example of a plane which sets off one degree off course then before long it is in a totally different place from where it wants to be. In the same way with tennis every degree you are off course to begin with throws you further out over time.

GET SOME COACHING!

I recall when I was about twenty three, being in a conversation with three senior managers at my work, who were a lot older than me who all played golf. They said to me that if I was to take up golf now it would be vital that the first thing I did would be to get coaching as I was so old! This was something I would always remember because I was fairly young but was being talked about as being old. It is of course the best advice that can be given for anyone taking up any sport at any age.

When I was twenty five I challenged my mixed doubles tennis partner to a game of squash. I knew she was a county standard squash player but being super confident in my ability at any racket sport, despite having only played squash eleven times in my whole life, I felt upbeat going into the match, feeling I could win. After all, she was four and a half months pregnant at the time, so I surely had to have a chance. After I came off the squash court having been beaten by three games to one I felt like I was about to have a heart attack as I had been running around so much, indeed it was the most shattered I have ever felt in my life. I even suspected that the one game that I did win (which I oddly won 9-0) had been thrown by her to not make me feel so bad, even though I hardly noticed any difference in her play compared to the other games. She was very modest but eventually I persuaded her to reveal to me just how good she was by telling me the best result she had ever had. She replied quite casually that, "well, I have beaten the number one player in Denmark". At this point I asked for a rematch and was squarely put in my place. She smiled at me and said, "Get some coaching first and then we'll have another game". Again it's one of those times you don't forget but she made a very good point – get some coaching!

11 YOU AND YOUR NEW POSITIVE ATTITUDE

ALWAYS GETTING SOMETHING POSITIVE OUT OF A MATCH

There are occasions in tennis when one player will play against another player who is considerably better and no matter what he tries he is just not good enough to beat him. In this scenario there will be a point in the match, for example in the second set, when the weaker player realises this and his head goes down. Very often the match just drifts away from him and the time he remains on court is wasted. Instead of getting nothing from this period (i.e. between the realisation of loss and the end of the match) it is worth the weaker player using this time to practice his shots.

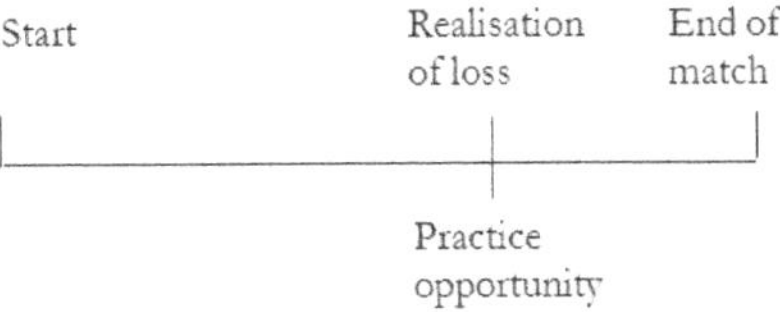

I would re-iterate that players should never give up, however if the match is not of great consequence then it is a good opportunity to try out things that a player might have practised in training but has not had chance to try out in a match situation. It is an opportunity to get something positive out of the game.

A player may decide that regardless of whom he is playing against and regardless of the importance of the match, he is going to force himself to practice a certain shot. An example was given earlier in the book about how I banned myself from playing a backhand slice and played only backhand topspins for a whole season. The point being made here is that as long as the player's technique is correct then the shot being practised should steadily improve. This means that regardless of the match result, the player has taken something positive from the match.

Practising new shots or adjusting techniques can also help with enjoying your tennis more as you will look forward to playing in the next match as you can try out your new shot.

THE CONSTRUCTION OF POSITIVITY

The way in which this book is different is that we concentrate on the positives. Let's look at a simple example. Imagine you have been knocking up against an opponent and he appears to be a superb player (we've all come across these players at some time), just think to yourself, "He can't be that good otherwise he would be playing at Wimbledon" or even, "He must have weaknesses in his game otherwise he would be playing at county level". It's only a simple statement but in your mind it is a positive known fact and it therefore creates the first solid step in your path to beating the opponent.

Another example of positive thought or 'thinking outside the box' is that if you hit the ball hard enough and in the correct place then it removes the whole concept of an opponent. If even the number one player in the world wouldn't be able to get to the shot you have just hit (because it's physically impossible) then the player you are up against certainly cannot. It is effectively in your control therefore and is just about you. The opponent who you have never beaten can't do a thing about the ball you have just hit. It is irrelevant how well he can hit the ball because he can't get there.

There is a great phrase from a well known film which is, "Fear? That's the other guy's problem!". Don't just read this phrase and forget it. Think about it, as it moves all the fear away from you and over to the other end of the court. An equivalent statement is, "Never mind any of my weaknesses, let's just concentrate on exploiting my opponent's weaknesses – he's got plenty of them".

WHAT OTHER EXPERTS SAY

- Dr Ann Quinn, the LTA's head of Sports Science in the UK in 2007, spoke to 'ACE magazine' and gave the following advice, "A positive attitude breeds positive experiences. One of the quickest ways to change your thinking is to mix with people who think in a positive way. Their outlook will rub off on you. Successful people leave clues. Confident individuals are doers and think in terms of challenges".
- In 'Tennis' a book by Van Raalte and Silver-Bernstein they comment, "Research shows that the less negative you are, the more likely you are to win. To put it another way, usually a match is one against one. When you are negative, it becomes two (your opponent and your negativity) against one (you)".
- John F Murray in his book 'Smart Tennis' states, "Achievement behaviour is traditionally seen as influenced by a blend of hope for success and fear of failure. In some sports, some athletes are primarily motivated to succeed, while others are more inspired to avoid failure. Take a moment to consider which of these two possibilities motivates you the most. Does hope for success or fear of failure lead to higher levels of motivation for you?".
- Murray also says, "Athletes who approach success derive great satisfaction from the pursuit without worrying about the possibility of failure. They are success orientated! They may become bored against much weaker opponents and apathetic when they have little chance of winning – but when the battle heats up, these are

> the real competitors. In my opinion, it's very important to develop a motivation to succeed because it gives you a focus that is positive, goal orientated, and anxiety reducing. Excessive fear of failure is a great impediment to success."

There can be days where you might not be up for a match but these are the ones that are worth your full effort as you need to believe that if you can win, the enthusiasm and love for the game will return and you will be motivated positively for future matches. It is worth toughing it out more than ever at this point.

Respected coach Patrick Mouratoglou, who runs his own tennis academy near Paris comments, "The most beautiful and difficult victories are those won on a day when everything seems difficult against an inferior opponent"

The reason most people play sport is for that exhilarating feeling of victory, whether they are aware of this or not. Keep fighting for that next win.

HOW TO GO ABOUT FEELING MORE POSITIVE

- When you go on court you need to think positively, make your mind up that this is what you are going to do. Why not force yourself to go on the attack more and keep attacking? Also when playing with others or running a team in any sport then remember the golden rule, "always give positive feedback to athletes".
- Using visual imagery is key in positive thinking and one excellent way of enhancing it further is by listening to your favourite motivational music

which will make the images seem much more inspirational. We all have songs that remind us of a particular good time in our lives and the uplifting power of music can be used alongside visual imagery to great benefit. So the next time you are driving to a match why not listen to motivational music on the way there; picture yourself playing on court as you listen to the music and think about how good you look on court and picture the superb winners that you are hitting. By the time you arrive for the match you will be desperate to get onto court and get at the opponent.

- Pick out positives from the small details so, for example, when your opponent misses two shots in a row, say to yourself, "this guy is a having a bad day".
- You might be a player who subconsciously thinks about the statistics. If you do then you need to ensure you are looking at the glass as being half full, not half empty. Let's say you win eight points in a row and then lose the next two. So do you look at this as having lost 100% of your last two points or winning an impressive 80% of your last ten points. Although I doubt many of us think in this way it merely goes to show how a positive slant can be applied to most situations when you look at the detail.
- We have already covered turning players, who come to matches with a negative mindset, into having a positive one. This is by thinking back to a positive match where everything went well. You too can do this for yourself before going on court. Why not write down a short list of all the

positive times. If you re-read this before a match then in a very short space of time you will be in a very positive place.

- Always try to pick some plus points for the upcoming match. The sun is shining, the courts have recently been resurfaced so the bounce is even, you are playing with a brilliant partner, you have brand new tennis balls. All these things can assist you in playing 'pure tennis' when you go on court.
- Improved physical fitness gives you more confidence on court. For example when I see a very overweight player across the net from me then it gives me a great psychological boost. Immediately I want to test his speed at getting to drop shots, to do body serves to see if he has difficulty moving to the side to play the shot and I also want to keep the ball in court as much as possible to make sure that by halfway through the match his fitness is being severely tested.

One point I will make is this. You need to work towards a goal of expecting success. Whether in tennis or in life, this begins with valuing yourself highly.

12 TOURNAMENTS

PREPARATION

Preparing well works on two fronts; ensuring firstly you have all the necessary tools with you to get through the tournament, and secondly when you have your house in order, you have greatly reduced the likelihood of negative thoughts popping into your head before or during a match. For those who prepare well for a tournament there is a fine line sometimes between doing certain tasks because they need to be done, doing them out of superstition or just because it makes the person feel better. The reason is unimportant just as long as you actually do it. If it is possible to remove current worries before the tournament or worries that you know you will have during the tournament and this can be done before the tournament, then only a fool would fail to remove them.

Preparation can be split into three levels as shown below. The list here can also be used by you as a quick reference before any tournament you are playing in, so it might be an idea to bookmark this page for future reference. It might also be an idea to get a pen now and add in any other key things you want to remember to do before a tournament that you think of as you are going through the list.

LEVEL 1 - THE ESSENTIALS

Enter yourself and your partner into the tournament in plenty of time. I have run tournaments before where a week after the tournament has been played people have rung me up to ask to be entered in the tournament that had already been and gone, despite it being well advertised. Ensure you have the following:

- First choice racket (with strings that are not about to break) and spare racket.
- Tournament entry fee and spare money.
- Method of getting there and back.
- Directions.
- Start Time and Date (double check!).
- The necessary kit. I played in a men's match recently when my partner and I played on an outdoor sandy all-weather court and he was wearing indoor trainers. He slipped and fell eight times in four sets. No one else went over at all. You get the point. Also make sure your trainers have good grips in case it rains. Don't allow any chance for your opponent to have an advantage.
- Work out the time you need to set off and then plan to leave ten minutes earlier than this time.

If you are to arrive early at any event then a tournament is definitely the place to do it as it gives you chance to ensure you know the rules and have a warm up.

LEVEL 2 - THE IMPORTANT STUFF

The next level includes ensuring you have the following:

- Food and drink. The tournament may last for many hours and you need to assume that there is no food and drink available.
- Practice balls.
- Cap (blinding sun can cost you the match. Before anyone says it's the same for everyone; it's not if your opponent has a cap and you don't). Bring a spare cap in case your partner needs one.
- Sunglasses if you are able to play in them – don't test out whether you can play in sunglasses for the first time in a tournament.
- Tracksuit top/sweater and trousers/pants to keep warm when you are off court, to reduce the likelihood of injuries when going back on court.
- Check the weather forecast so you have an idea of whether there is likely to be wind, rain or sun.
- Eat the correct food for the twenty four hours leading up to the tournament.
- Rest the day before. Playing a four hour match in the sun the day before a tournament increases the likelihood that you will come up short in the latter stages of the tournament should you get that far. If you do well enough in the

tournament to reach the final, then one of the key thoughts you should be thinking at the time is that you are fitter than your opponent at that particular point and therefore have a crucial advantage over him. If you are exhausted at the point of walking onto the court in the final then the whole thing could well be a bit of a waste of time.

- To improve your performance in the rain the crucial aspect is having trainers with good grips. A useful tip is to always keep a new pair of trainers with you, for example leave them permanently in the boot of your car, and if it starts raining switch trainers to this new pair. As these new trainers don't get as much use as your usual pair (because they are only brought out in the rain) they will retain their grips for longer and will be crucial in ensuring you don't end up slipping and sliding in the wet. In the next match when you have a dry surface you can switch back to the trainers which do not have quite the same level of grip as the new trainers, assuming they have sufficient of course..

LEVEL 3 – COMPLETE PREPARATION

These are all the things that you need to do in order to ensure there is nothing left that you could worry about. The aim is that having completed these tasks and by having these items with you, you are able to satisfy yourself that there will be nobody at the tournament who is better prepared than you are. There might be one or two who are equally well prepared but as far as preparation and having your house in order, you are the number one.

This list will always vary from person to person but I have highlighted some of mine which range from being sensible to being a little extreme.

- For an early afternoon tournament I want to have had two meals beforehand so that I know I can last the tournament without needing to eat much during it. I rise at 8:30am therefore and have a breakfast high in protein, my usual being boiled eggs, milk and toast. The background behind my eating a high protein diet before a tennis match came from when I was younger. I would often go a little dizzy on court after only a few minutes so decided to go to the doctor. He told me to eat this meal before a game. Sure enough it was like a miracle cure. It was then that I realised how massive the effect of diet is. At about noon I then have a small to medium size warm meal including meat and veg.
- A few weeks before, I would order a few tennis shirts that are the same make and style the professionals wear. I would wear my favourite one for the tournament and ensure that my clothes were clean, ironed and matching. You don't always know what goes on in an opponent's head but he can often give away points early on in a match just because he has a perceived idea in his head about you. I always like to present a fresh enthusiastic appearance. If instead you turn up looking like you have just walked off a football pitch then it gives your opponent a lift.

- Ensure everything is ready the day before the tournament so nothing needs to be done on the actual day. Life is such that it throws up problems at the most inopportune times so giving yourself leeway is a good idea.
- Watch tennis videos to aid visual imagery.
- Listen to motivational/uplifting music on the way to the match.
- Get a good nights sleep the night before.
- Removing clutter reduces tension. Do you feel better when your room is tidier, your car is clean? If so do these tasks before the day of the tournament.
- Tim Henman advises that it is sensible to get a sweat on as you are walking onto the court, for example, by doing some jogging beforehand. This would usually be achieved by a good warm up though.

One thing to consider is that if you are doing all this preparation for a tournament then others in the tournaments you enter may well be doing the same. If you are prepared yourself then you can at least guarantee no one else will have an advantage by being better prepared than you.

DEALING WITH NERVES IN A FINAL

People have different techniques on how to deal with a pressure match. When Pete Sampras reached his first Wimbledon final, he discovered a way to deal with nerves which was to kid his mind into believing he wasn't in the final at all and in fact wasn't even at Wimbledon. He pretended that the match was just the first round in Cincinnati. This method worked perfectly and going forward he took this thinking into each final.

In Jeff Greenwald's book 'The Best Tennis of Your Life' he says, "I've been asked how the best players in the world compete so well when the stakes are so high. How do players deal with the stress with so much on the line? Answer: They learn to thrive on it.". The title of the first chapter in his book encapsulates this very important message, 'Find Pleasure in Pressure'.

Greenwald goes onto comment, "You need to understand that your tension is actually the catalyst to peak performance. You need it. Without it, your best tennis will not emerge. Do not be scared of it; use it. Breathe and smile to yourself as you decide to channel this energy into the ball. It simply means that you care and are excited to be in this moment. Next time you go 5-4 up in the third set serving, feel a pang of nervous energy, and find yourself hoping your opponent will hand you the match with some loose errors, remind yourself, "I love this. I wouldn't want to be anywhere else".".

IMAGERY

Sports psychologists advise that mental imagery can be of great benefit. By imagining glorious winning shots, or playing in front of a crowd you are mentally preparing yourself for when the situation arises. In 'Sport Psychology' Matt Jarvis explains, "when we imagine carrying out a sporting technique, the nervous system and muscles react in a similar manner to that expected if we were actually carrying out the technique. Another reason mental rehearsal works is that it desensitises us to the anxiety of competitive situations. The more we are exposed to things that cause us anxiety - whether in real-life or in our imagination – the less anxiety they cause".

There are two ways of using visual imagery. Firstly, from an internal perspective, as if you are looking through your own eyes and secondly, from an external perspective, as though you are watching yourself on video. Think about a scenario where you are playing a match and are standing at the net and your opponent has directed a shot at your body so you can see this ball coming straight at you. Look at it through your own eyes and visualise punching the volley away from your opponent for a winner. Now watch exactly the same point but instead of watching it through your eyes as the player on the court, look at it through the eyes of a friend who is standing by the net post watching you punch the same volley away. It's an interesting concept to be able to switch views as though you were playing a computer game.

So which is the best form of imagery to use – internal (your eyes) or external (through the eyes of your friend on the sideline)? Well the answer is both. You need to use each one for different shots. When you play a volley your tennis racket is never behind you so is always in your sight (even if it is only peripheral for some of it), throughout the period from preparing the volley to executing it. This means that using internal imagery, so looking through your own eyes, is the best form of visual imagery to use as you are used to seeing the whole shot. However when you are trying to visualise your ground stokes or serve it is better to use external imagery (through your friends eyes) because when you take your racket back preparing for the shot you have your eyes on the ball and not on the racket. The same applies on the follow through. The friend at the side-line therefore can see your full racket swing whereas 'imaging' it through your own eyes will mean that you will not include the backswing or the follow through which is a large part of the shot that is being played.

Visual imagery is a technique used right across all professional sports. Former footballer Gianfranco Zola, who was a free kick specialist, explained the reason behind the number of goals he scored from set pieces, "The success I have at free kicks is 5 per cent skill and 95 per cent successful imagery".

A highly successful Olympic Springboard diver stated:

"I did my dives in my head all the time. At night, before going to sleep, I always did my dives. Ten dives. I started with a front dive, the first one I had to do at the Olympics, and I did everything as if I was actually there. I saw myself on the board with the same bathing suit. Everything was the same. I saw myself in the pool at the Olympics doing my dives. If the dive was wrong, I went back and started over again. It takes a good hour to do perfect imagery of all of my dives, but for me it was better than a workout. Sometimes I would take the weekend off and do imagery five times a day. I felt like I was on the board and I did each dive so many times in my mind.

It took me a long time to control my images and perfect my imagery, maybe a year, doing it every day. At first I couldn't see myself, I always saw someone else, or I would see my dives wrong all the time. I would get an image of hurting myself, or tripping on the board, or I would see something done really bad. As I continued to work on it, I got to the point where I could see myself doing the perfect dive and the crowd yelling at the Olympics. But it took me a long time. I read everything I had to do and I knew my dive by heart. Then I started to see myself on the board doing my perfect dive. But some days I couldn't see it, or it was a bad dive in my head. I worked at it so much it got to the point that I could do all my dives easily".

The last example shows the level of professionalism involved if you wish to operate at the very highest level. As far as the local club player is concerned it is unlikely that you will work at imagery quite this intensely, however it is a proven technique that should be tried.

Close your eyes now and 'image' exactly how each one of your shots looks when played to perfection. Do this from an internal and external perspective. If you are able to video record yourself on court playing your actual shots, then watch this back as this helps with external 'imaging'.

THOUGHTS OF BEING TOP DOG

If you are good enough, the opposition is bad enough or you manage to get yourself a brilliant partner (always a favourite of mine) then you may win a trophy or two.

This is a great feeling to have as it gives you a great psychological boost to be able to walk onto the court for the next year knowing that you are the club's or league's champion. If you manage this then say to yourself in your head that you are a champion, it will undoubtedly give you a lift.

LOSING

So not everything has gone to plan and instead of winning you have lost. My advice to you is to lose gracefully. As well as others thinking better of you for it, there is another reason. I recently played in a team that won the cup final we had reached. It was a close contest and our opponents had got themselves psyched up into thinking that they were going to win their first trophy for a couple of years. As the match neared the end we were running out of light and had to move to a different venue. The opposition were very aggrieved that they had been having to play in fading light and had got very angry with me as I had selected the original venue which didn't have floodlights. I am entirely sure that the fading light had no effect on the result as it was the same for both sides. However when we finally beat them we got a lot of complaints from them to the point where it completely ruined the enjoyment of winning the cup. It very much ruined for us what was a great achievement. So the second reason for you to lose graciously is so that the opposition can enjoy their win, as one day it will be you on the winning side and you want to be able to enjoy it too.

If you lose a match and someone asks, "What happened?", then don't start explaining, just pay a compliment about your opponent (not too complimentary) and change the subject. If you start telling others about your poor backhand or that you struggled under pressure then these statements are printed in hardback in your's and others' minds especially if the person you have said it to then tells others which they will often do. Keep your thoughts inside your own head. In time they will slip away and you will forget about them. That isn't to say though that they should be ignored and not worked upon for future tournaments.

USEFUL TIPS

- The best tip possible is to get the strongest partner you can to play with as this gives you the best chance of doing well.
- If it's very sunny then drink plenty of liquid and stay in the shade in between matches – the sun will sap your energy and you need to assume that you will need that energy in the later stages of the tournament.
- The next point I learnt in the most painful way possible. I had entered a mixed doubles tournament which had varying standards of pairs in it including a gentlemen who I knew to be a very competent player who had decided to enter with his wife, who was considerably weaker. It was a round robin tournament and he took me to the side and asked if we would go easy on them as his wife wasn't that strong. My opponent was a gentleman and I acceded to his

wishes. The format of the tournament was to play ten games against each of the other pairs, we won this particular match 7-3 as we didn't play flat out. As the tournament progressed we beat all but one of the other pairs who we drew 5-5 with. The two pairs who scored the most games in the tournament qualified for the final however despite all our good results, it was not us. One of the pairs, who we had beaten, qualified instead of us as they had been ruthless in their game against the pair with the weak lady and had won 10-0. We missed out on qualifying for the final by one game. The gentleman, mentioned previously, came up to me upon realising what had happened and apologised for asking us to go easy on them but I could do nothing but assure him it wasn't his fault. I wished the ground would swallow me up. Needless to say, that after that I never made the same mistake again and would fight for every game I played. I also told every partner I entered the tournament with in the years after that what had happened. This had the desired effect that I wanted in the tournament the year after as towards the end of the group stage my partner turned to me and said that she couldn't stop thinking about the story I had told her.

- If you are not feeling confident on a particular aspect of your game then try to play the shots you are comfortable with and play yourself into the tournament. As you and your strokes get warmed up the shots you were not as confident about will start to flow.

- When you are one of the favourites in a tournament you will often have other strong pairs watching you to assess your strengths and weaknesses. I have always found this a great boost to my confidence, having the main opponents trying to work me out, so by the same logic I always make sure that if I am evaluating other strong pairs in a tournament that I don't make it obvious. If a strong opponent starts believing that you hold them in even the smallest amount of respect then you are giving them a psychological head start in the match.

SUMMARY

It is important in a tournament to have no fear, yet have nerves. It is important to not be arrogant. One of the best things about tournament play though is the excitement you can feel before and during it. If you are just starting out playing tournaments then you may not feel this because nerves may be the overriding emotion, however just keep entering more tournaments. You will start to feel more comfortable playing tournaments the more you enter, and you will soon love the rush that goes with them too.

BIBLIOGRAPHY

REFERENCE MATERIAL

Borg Versus McEnroe (2005) – Malcolm Folley
The Inner Game of Tennis (1975) – W.Timothy Gallwey
Sport Psychology (1999) – Matt Jarvis
Serious (2002) – John McEnroe
Winning Ugly (2007) – Brad Gilbert
Lifting the Covers (2005) – Alan Mills
Holding Serve – Michael Chang
Ace Magazine (various editions)
Lawn Tennis Courtcraft (1964) – N H Patterson
Think to win (1993) – Allen Fox
British Tennis Coaches Association website (2007) Dave Sammell
Social Tennis (2000) - Jake Barnes
Sport Psychology Library: Tennis (1999) – Judy L. Van Raalte and Carrie Silver-Bernstein
Smart Tennis – John F Murray
How to Succeed at tennis (1979) – Peter Scholl
Tennis Psychology (1976) – Harold Geist and Cecilia A.Martinez
The Anatomy and Psychology of Tennis (1966) – R.A.Fish
The Little Book of Calm (1996) – Paul Wilson
Overcoming Anger and Irritability – William Davies
The Best Tennis of Your Life – Jeff Greenwald

RECOMMENDED READING

The Inner Game of Tennis (1975) – W.Timothy Gallwey

ABOUT THE AUTHOR

Adrian Lobley currently lives in Leeds. He has played tennis since the age of 11 primarily at Bardsey Tennis Club but has also been a member at Chapel Allerton, Rawdon and Wetherby tennis clubs in Yorkshire, and Chesham Bois and Chorleywood in Buckinghamshire and Hertfordshire.

He first took an interest in running tennis teams at the age of 16 when he ran Bardsey's junior mixed team, and then followed that by running Bardsey's senior mixed team a year later. During his time in charge of the senior team it won promotion from Division 4 to Division 1, and won two Division 1 titles and two league cups in the Barkston Ash league. Adrian had a period away from Bardsey for three years where he ran Rawdon's mixed first-team, winning the Leeds League Division 1 title. He has managed teams for 22 of the last 25 years and has not yet suffered relegation. Adrian also enters mixed and men's doubles tournaments with a number of different tennis partners. He has appeared in 17 regional doubles finals and has finished on the winning side on all 17 occasions. His longest tie-break winning streak is 23 tie-breaks in a row.

Adrian is currently struggling with repetitive strain injury in his right arm, and is now learning to play left-handed in the hope of continuing to play the game he loves.

CPSIA information can be obtained at www.ICGtesting.com
Printed in the USA
LVOW05s1447201114

414759LV00019B/855/P